Any Fool Can
Complete an Acquisition

Any Fool Can Complete an Acquisition

The Harsh Reality Is Most Acquisitions
Do Not Live Up to Expectations

It Doesn't Have to Be This Way

Glenn Personey

Vision, Strategy, and M&A Best Practices

Vision, Strategy, and M&A Best Practices

ISBN 979-8-9871209-0-3 (E-book)

ISBN 979-8-9871209-1-0 (Paperback)

Library of Congress Control Number: 2022919139

First Edition. First published in Dallas, Texas

Please recognize that vision, strategy, and M&A transactions are inherently uncertain due to events or combinations of events that cannot be foreseen, including but not limited to actions by the counterparty, regulators, industry, government, individuals, new entrants in the industry, market forces, and the people in your company, all of which may affect outcomes and results.

You should also engage a knowledgeable attorney when undertaking M&A transactions.

I very much hope this book becomes a valuable resource in your vision, strategy, and M&A success!

Glenn Personey
(316) 619-7868
https://www.personeymallc.com

Glenn is available for advisory work related to vision, strategy, and M&A transactions. Call (316) 619-7868 to discuss what you would like assistance with.

Why Read This Book

The best practices discussed in this book will help you identify and complete the most attractive transactions, generate exceptional results, and simultaneously build your firm's vision, strategy, and M&A capability.

Many of these concepts and principles are unlike anything you have experienced before and have been proven to improve transaction success. They will do the same for your company.

This is not an academic exercise. A successful acquisition, for example, can create hundreds of millions of dollars in value. Conversely, a failed acquisition can put the entire company at risk.

You will be shocked and pleasantly surprised at what you can accomplish when using the best practices discussed in this book.

Written by a Vision, Strategy, and M&A Executive

Glenn's insights are based on over forty years of experience leading transactions, negotiating agreements, developing successful strategies, and building vision, strategy, and M&A capability while working at:

- Flint Hills Resources, LLC: a subsidiary of Koch Industries, Inc., one of the largest privately held companies in America.
- Clark Refining and Marketing, Inc., which was owned by private equity.
- Conoco Inc., which was a Fortune 500 company.
- Helping clients as an independent consultant.

During his career, he has led over $5 billion of acquisitions and divestitures, negotiated complex joint ventures, negotiated over 200 commercial agreements, restructured major companies, launched M&A and Business Development groups, and led Vision & Strategy Reset initiatives for multiple companies.

After retiring from Flint Hills Resources, Glenn founded Personey M&A Consulting and began helping senior executives and business owners dramatically improve their results using the best practices contained in this book.

Acknowledgments

My perspectives were developed while working for three excellent companies, all of which encouraged entrepreneurship:

- Conoco Inc.
- Clark Refining and Marketing, Inc.
- Flint Hills Resources, LLC: a subsidiary of Koch Industries, Inc.

Further insights were gained while helping clients as an independent consultant.

Special thanks to Alex Snyder, my former M&A colleague and founder of the Crimson Fulcrum Strategic Institute; Dan Appelbaum, my former M&A colleague at Clark Refining and Marketing, Inc., and Jim Lahey, my former management colleague at Conoco Inc., who devoted their personal time to reading the book and providing valuable input.

A special thanks goes out to Richard Nongard, who offered the information required to transform this book from a written draft into the final product, as well as to my editors Ita de Groot and Tamelynda Lux. Please note any errors or omissions are entirely my responsibility.

Preface

A long time ago, I started competing to win.

Along the way, it became clear there was a better way.

Now my goal is to help **you** succeed.

Table of Contents

The harsh reality is most vision, strategy, and M&A transactions (acquisitions, divestitures, mergers, and joint ventures) do not live up to expectations. It doesn't have to be this way.

Inadequate vision or poorly executed transactions cause hardship, destruction of market value, and ruined careers.

You know it's true. You were there when your company did not know what was needed to succeed due to inadequate vision or was headed into a destructive transaction because of poor M&A practices.

Over time it became clear that many traditional concepts concerning vision, strategy, and M&A did not deliver exceptional results and, in some cases, resulted in outright failure.

The best practices discussed in this book offer an entirely new perspective, which was developed by observing what works and, equally importantly, what does not. They have consistently produced superior results and created significant value.

Resetting your Vision & Strategy is the first step you should take before beginning any M&A activity. Many companies skip this step and go off the rails from the start.

Chapter 5: Transaction Best Practices

Transaction Best Practices are fact-based, focused, and use emotional intelligence. They have been shown to deliver superior M&A results and are presented in the form of a success wheel with four primary elements:

- *Vision & Target Screening*
- *Diligence Focus & Deal Team Dynamics*
- *Upfront Agreement & Negotiation Style*
- *Build M&A Capability in Your Firm*

Chapter 6: Additional Lessons

Additional lessons that are vital for your M&A success are covered in this portion of the book. The material is grouped into the following *categories:*

- *Effective Negotiations*
- *Acquisition Integration*
- *Diagnose M&A Failures*
- *Business Optimization*
- *Questions You Should Ask when Approached to Invest*
- *All Companies Can Build M&A Capability*

Chapter 7: Nontraditional Economic Analysis

Sometimes the best acquisitions are the ones you don't make. Nontraditional economic analysis will allow you to quickly eliminate potential acquisition targets that do not measure up to other alternatives and stress test those with the greatest promise.

These principles and techniques are discussed in the following sections:

- *Qualitative Screening Tools*
- *High-Level Quantitative Metrics*
- *Approach with Clear-Eyed Realism*

The Cold Eye Review is significantly underutilized because it requires humility and willingness to accept challenge. You must recognize that your team does not know everything, and be willing to accept challenge from a person outside your organization.

A Cold Eye Review is a powerful tool. Your transaction success will improve when you recognize that an outside perspective will bring impartial and valuable insight. It is in your best interests to listen.

Once the deal euphoria fades, all that remains is your working relationship with the counterparty (which can change) and the transaction documents (which are fixed).

Take the time to review this section in detail. It supplies valuable reference material to help you successfully negotiate and draft your transaction documents including:

- *Acquisition and Divestiture Term Sheet Preparation*
- *Joint Venture Term Sheet Preparation*
- *Confidential Information Memorandum Preparation*

Toolbox is devoted to specific tools and templates referred to in earlier discussions that will help you during the M&A process.

The Strategy Reset and M&A Best Practices discussed in this book have helped widely diverse companies develop dramatic new visions, execute actionable strategies, and complete highly successful transactions.

Now that you have been through the book, I recommend you reexamine the case studies originally presented in Chapter 4: Vision & Strategy Reset, through the lens of your new knowledge and perspective.

Now is your opportunity to make a significant difference in the company's prospects and the lives of the people who work there!

You will be shocked and pleasantly surprised at what you can accomplish using the principles and techniques discussed in this book.

Chapter 1
A New Perspective

Across the table were senior executives for Chevron Refining, Chevron Chemical, Chevron Legal, and three of their outside M&A attorneys.

Clark Refining and Marketing was represented by me, a very young VP of Refining Business Development and Strategy, along with two outside M&A attorneys.

We were negotiating to purchase a Chevron refinery in Port Arthur, Texas, and the discussions were not going well. Chevron thought they would simply use a win-lose strategy and run over us.

Their negotiation positions included aggressive environmental liability transfer and one-sided feedstock supply and service agreements. They also showed no interest in being flexible on any proposed terms.

Believing the discussion would be a waste of time, I started packing up, indicating their positions were unacceptable and that they should find another purchaser.

To my surprise, they asked for a private conference among themselves. When they returned, the question was, "What would you accept?"

My response was to lay out a list of everything we wanted, which was significantly more than I would have requested under different circumstances.

After another private conference, they returned and accepted all the major points in my counterproposal, so we continued moving forward with acquisition discussions.

Ultimately, Clark was able to purchase the refinery for $76 million plus inventory, turn it around and create an asset valued at $2–3 billion before making any significant new capital investments.

It was then I realized that virtually all the conventional wisdom concerning M&A negotiations was incorrect, and the field was wide open for developing a new approach.

Chapter 2
Conventional M&A Underperforms

Inadequate vision and poorly executed transactions cause hardship, destruction of market value, and ruined careers.

You know it's true.

You were there when your company did not know what was needed to succeed due to inadequate vision or was headed into a destructive transaction because of poor M&A practices.

It is discouraging for everyone when results do not meet expectations, competitors outmaneuver you, and acquisitions underperform.

At the extreme, some companies have declared bankruptcy or have been liquidated because of these failures. You can easily think of several household names.

What makes it worse is the feeling of hopelessness because a clear path to overcoming these problems is not readily apparent.

The harsh reality is that most vision, strategy, and M&A transactions do not live up to expectations.

It doesn't have to be this way.

This is the genesis of this book.

Chapter 3
True Best Practices Excel

Over time it became clear that many traditional concepts concerning vision, strategy, and M&A did not deliver exceptional results and, in some cases, resulted in outright failure.

The best practices discussed in this book offer an entirely new perspective, which was developed by observing what works and, equally importantly, what does not. They have consistently produced superior results and created significant value.

You now have a choice between continuing with a marginal vision, declining prospects, and protecting the status quo or transforming your company with a clear vision, actionable strategies, and exceptional M&A results.

The central concepts discussed in this book are briefly outlined below to give you a feel for the topics and the extent of the material included.

The Vision & Strategy Reset portion of the book provides a comprehensive guide for resetting the vision of your company, which is the first step you should take before beginning any M&A activity. Many companies skip this step and go off the rails from the start.

The M&A Best Practices portion of the book provides a comprehensive guide for successfully growing your business through transactions such as acquisitions, divestitures, joint ventures, and mergers.

Many of the concepts and principles discussed in this book are unlike anything you have experienced before and have been proven to improve transaction success.

Chapter 4
Vision & Strategy Reset

Vision & Strategy Reset is a comprehensive guide for resetting the vision and strategy of your company which is the first step you should take before beginning any M&A activity.

To accomplish this, you must envision what your business can become and develop realistic strategies to make it happen.

A successful Strategy Reset can easily create hundreds of millions of dollars in value. This is not an academic exercise.

The following is an outline of the material that will be covered in this section:

- *Introduction*
- *Reset Roadmap*
- *Vision & Strategy Reset - Flowchart*
- *Proposed Solution*
- *Vision & Strategy Wheel*
- *Industry Value Creation*
- *Long-Term Macro Perspectives*
- *Competitor & Market Analysis*
- *Black Swan Events: Historical & Future*
- *Capability Evaluation*

- *Financial Analysis of Value Chains & Strategy Economics*
- *Goals*
- *Case Studies*
- *Long-Term, Fact-Based, Strategic Thinking*

INTRODUCTION

Resetting your Vision & Strategy is the first step you should take before beginning any M&A activity, including acquisitions, divestitures, mergers, and joint ventures. Many companies skip this step and go off the rails from the start.

Why? Because any transaction can look attractive without a well-thought-out vision with actionable strategies.

You should also reset your vision and strategies if:

- You are entering a new industry.
- The company is facing major challenges.
- Your current strategy is not delivering the results you are looking for.

This process is designed to develop new out-of-the-box thinking that will contribute significant earnings growth rather than making minor incremental improvements.

To accomplish this, you must envision what your business can become and not allow limited availability of capital, existing staffing levels, or current organizational expertise limit your thinking. If the strategy is sound, all of this can be secured.

The major sections of a Strategy Reset are shown in the flowchart on page 13. Notice the deliverables on the right side. The most successful Vision & Strategies:

- Improve competitive position.
- Contribute strongly to earnings.
- Do not leave money on the table.
- Have a reasonable risk profile.
- Create business optionality.
- Are unique and difficult to duplicate.

A "me too" strategy is a loser strategy; your competitor already owns this ground.

If a Vision & Strategy doesn't do these things, it won't create excellent results. For that matter, if it doesn't deliver these things, why are you wasting your time?

Amazing results can be achieved when you invite external challenge, remove internal barriers, and envision what the business could be rather than what it is today.

RESET ROADMAP

The following sections of the book explain the step-by-step roadmap for completing a Vision & Strategy Reset for your company.

Vision & Strategy Reset Flowchart

- Visual representation of the entire process

Proposed Solution

- Areas of specific recommendations

Strategy Reset Deliverables

- Vision & Strategy Wheel
- Action planning

Industry Value Creation

- Define the products and services that are needed to create the end product

Long-Term Macro Perspectives

- Identify long-term trends that may impact your industry
- Discover damaging trends and beneficial trends

Competitor & Market Analysis

- Understand the dynamics of your markets
- Recognize the strategies of your competitors

Black Swan Events: Historical & Future

- Envision what can happen and consider the potential impact

Capability Evaluation

- Identify the capabilities in your company that result in a competitive benefit
- Ascertain the capabilities needed to implement the new Vision & Strategies successfully

Financial Analysis of Value Chains & Strategy Economics

- Understand the profitability of different segments of your existing business
- Economic analysis of each proposed new strategy so you can select the best options

Goals

- Goals are set to ensure the scope of work will accomplish your objectives

Case Studies

- Successful Vision & Strategy Reset case studies

Long-Term, Fact-Based, Strategic Thinking

- You now have the tools to envision what your business can become

VISION & STRATEGY RESET – FLOWCHART

Industry Value Creation
(Understand the profitability of all products and services required to create the end product.)

Long-Term Macro Perspectives
(Identify long-term trends in society, technology, government and global affairs that may affect the industry.)

Competitor & Market Analysis
(Determine the dynamics of the markets and the strategies of major competitors.)

Black Swan Events
(Envision what can happen no matter how unlikely and consider the impact.)

Financial Analysis of Value Chains
(Define the profitability of the existing business segments.)

Strategy Economic Analysis
(Ascertain the relative economic positions of the different vision and strategy options.)

Capability Evaluation
(Consider existing capabilities and those that are required to achieve the new vision and strategies.)

Develop a Unified Vision with Actionable Strategies

The Most Successful Vision and Strategies:

- Improve competitive position
- Contribute strongly to earnings
- Do not leave money on the table
- Have a reasonable risk profile
- Create business optionality
- Are unique and difficult to duplicate

PROPOSED SOLUTION

The Vision and Strategy team should propose specific recommendations in three categories:

1) **Unified Vision:** options that will allow the company to deliver significant earnings growth over the next two to five years.

2) **Actionable Strategies:** new strategies for running your existing business and taking advantage of emerging opportunities in the marketplace.

3) **Capability Enhancement:** development of the skills and abilities needed to execute the new Vision & Strategies successfully.

VISION & STRATEGY WHEEL

The final Vision & Strategy Reset for your company will consider the results from all work modules taken as a unified whole, with each section contributing potential new strategies.

- Condense the results of the analysis into a Vision & Strategy Wheel:

  o A four or five-word vision (or theme) as the hub
  o Actionable strategies as the spokes
  o Existing business as well as new markets, products, and capabilities
  o Entirely new business platforms: upstream or downstream businesses
  o Growth

- Vision and strategies must meet the following requirements for the best chance of making a meaningful impact on the company's performance:

  o Improve your competitive position
  o Contribute significant earnings growth
  o Do not leave money on the table
  o Have a reasonable risk profile
  o Create business optionality
  o Are unique and difficult for your competitors to duplicate

- The results of the Strategy Reset process should be presented to your board or equivalent corporate decision-makers to get their input and decide on an action plan.

INDUSTRY VALUE CREATION

OVERVIEW

Assess industry value creation using a flowchart that shows the products and services needed to create the end product or service.

Identify average profitability for each step in the flowchart along with ease of entry into that segment of the value flow.

VALUE DEVELOPMENT

The value flowchart makes it straightforward to consider the relative profitability and concentration for each upstream and downstream product or service.

This directional analysis supplies helpful background material as you work through the Strategy Reset process.

Develop a value creation flowchart for your specific industry. The following is a generalized example:

INDUSTRY VALUE CREATION FLOWCHART

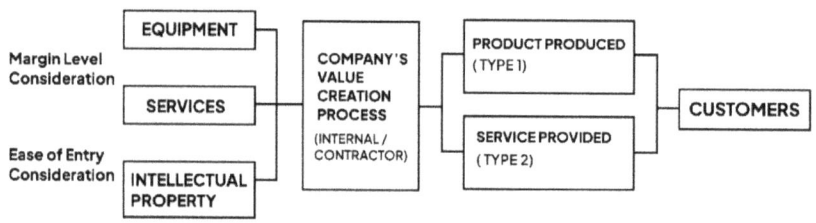

TACTICAL ACTION PLAN

- **Complete a value creation flowchart for your industry.** This should include your existing business, new products/services under development, and potential applications in other industries. Pay particular attention to each flowchart section's average margin and ease of entry.

- **Review all the work in this area** and decide what overall conclusions can be reached and specific strategies that may be most successful.

WHY IS THIS IMPORTANT?

Consider, for example, if large margins are realized by input providers (left side of the chart) or customers (right side of the chart), <u>and</u> it is easy to enter those industries.

In this situation, you might want to consider an upstream or downstream integration strategy, which could be conducted through an acquisition or expansion of your existing business.

LONG-TERM MACRO PERSPECTIVES

OVERVIEW

This step evaluates long-term trends that may affect your industry to find *resisters* (damaging trends) and *accelerators* (beneficial trends) that already exist or are ascending. The team developing these perspectives will only use factual data; opinions are excluded.

VALUE DEVELOPMENT

Going through this process will help you anticipate long-term macro changes that could materially impact your business.

LONG-TERM MACRO PERSPECTIVES – VISUAL

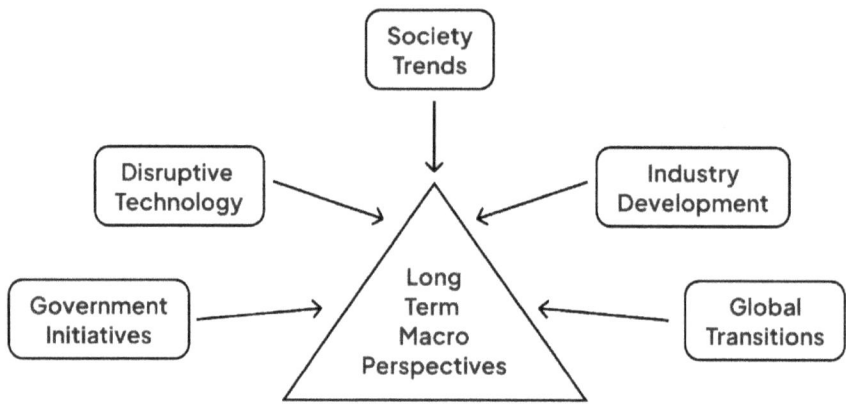

TACTICAL ACTION PLAN

- **Identify the primary markets in which your organization competes** and those where competitors offer services (e.g., product/service/geography). What changes are occurring?
- **Research disruptive technology developments in your industry.** Disruptive technology is an innovative

technology or process that delivers superior results at lower costs.

- **Explore societal trends** (e.g., climate change; aging of the population; increasing use of digital devices; artificial intelligence; big data; privacy laws; 3D printing; pandemic impact).
- **Examine new US government initiatives** (e.g., support for green energy; China tariffs; increasing government debt; changes in environmental regulations; changes in legal regulations; pandemic impact on strategic US manufacturing).
- **Investigate global transitions** (e.g., protectionism; regional rather than global supply chains; increasing government debt; China's aggressive behavior; recognition of Israel by the Arab world; regional conflicts).
- **Seek existing industry outlook publications** that are already available.
- **Identify resisters and accelerators** with respect to each of the work streams above.
- **Review all the work in this area** and decide what overall conclusions can be reached and specific strategies that may be most successful.

WHY IS THIS IMPORTANT?

- Most companies do not pay attention to long-term macro factors that could affect their industry. This is a significant shortcoming because the most serious long-term threats to an industry originate from the outside.
- Consider, for example, that most of the threats to printed news, computer mainframes, phone landlines, video cassette rentals, music CDs, and movie DVDs originated outside the industry.

COMPETITOR & MARKET ANALYSIS

OVERVIEW

The Competitor & Market Analysis strives to understand the dynamics of your markets and the strategies of all major competitors.

The analysis will identify qualitative and quantitative differences between competitors in your markets.

VISUAL EXAMPLE – COMPETITIVE ELEMENTS

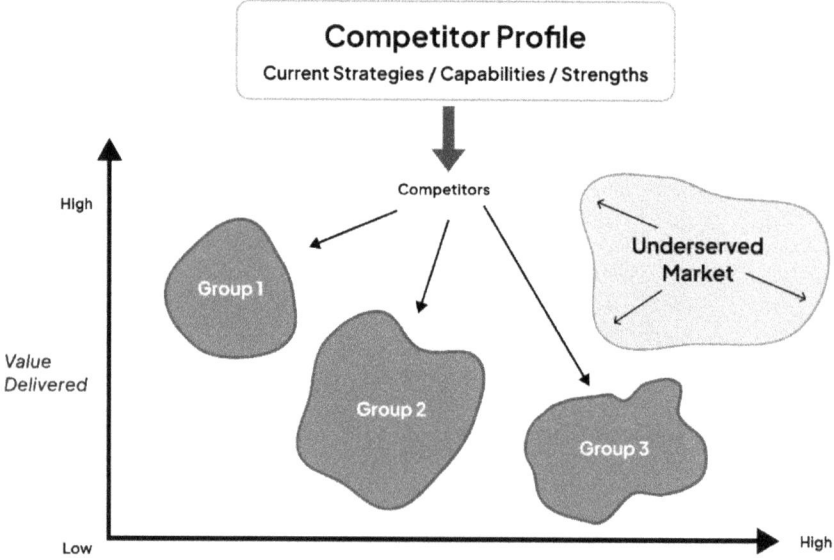

This is an example of a competitive elements graph built using qualitative factors.

VALUE DEVELOPMENT

The results of the analysis in this section can be eye-opening for your company and are a critical part of developing your overall vision and strategies.

You must understand your competitors and markets to develop a Vision & Strategy with the best chance of success.

TACTICAL ACTION PLAN

- **Complete the competitive elements graph shown above.** Create the graph so it is industry-specific, with your company and competitors plotted on it.
- **Prepare a position in the ocean graph.** Show purchaser value (low to high) and relative cost (low to high). Use price as a proxy for cost if this information is not available. ALDI versus Whole Foods is an example of this analysis.
- **Create a cost or price stack.** Operating costs or prices are shown on the vertical axis from low to high, and production capacity or market share is shown on the horizontal axis from low to high.
- **Understand your competitors.** What does each competitor say about your company when calling on a client? Are their statements true? Why do some customers believe them?
- **Benchmark other successful businesses in your industry.** Consider whether some of their programs may be options for your company. Use information available in the public domain, such as filings with the Securities and Exchange Commission (SEC) and investor presentations. Also, have discussions with companies willing to share their best practices.
- **Review all the work in this area** and decide what overall conclusions can be reached and specific strategies that may be most successful.

WHY IS THIS IMPORTANT?

The number of companies that do not understand their markets or competitors is shockingly large. A successful Vision & Strategy Reset requires a complete understanding of both.

BLACK SWAN EVENTS:
HISTORICAL & FUTURE

OVERVIEW

The Black Swan analysis will envision what can happen no matter how unlikely and consider the potential impact.

You should review historical Black Swan events and consider what may happen in the future.

VALUE DEVELOPMENT

Understanding the potential for Black Swan events to affect your proposed strategies (both positive and negative) is necessary to ensure you are not blindsided by a significant downside event or pass up a strategy with significant upside potential.

It is not possible to know the future, but it is possible to anticipate what might happen, consider the implications, and use this to create a competitive advantage.

Many historical Black Swan events could have been predicted by examining ongoing changes in the world and society (e.g., 911/2008 Financial Crisis/World War II/$100 barrel crude oil/Dot-com bubble/COVID-19 pandemic/Ukraine invasion).

TACTICAL ACTION PLAN

- **Develop a range of potential Black Swan events** and consider the impact on the proposed strategies. Examples might include: Another pandemic in five years; a 9.0 earthquake in California; new electric car battery technology that extends the driving range to 1,000 miles; Russia invading a NATO country, and China attacking Taiwan.
- **Review all the work in this area** and decide what overall conclusions can be reached and specific strategies that may be most successful.

Refine your choice of strategies to:

o   Remove those with significant downside potential.
o   Favor those with considerable upside potential.

WHY IS THIS IMPORTANT

Black Swan events can impact a company's profitability more than any other consideration. Pay attention to these potential benefits and risks when resetting your vision and strategies.

CAPABILITY EVALUATION

OVERVIEW

Capability evaluation identifies your company's competitive advantages. You should also identify the skills required to successfully implement the new vision and strategies.

DESCRIPTION

A company's capabilities should flow from organizational attributes rather than individual skills and be separate from the company's physical assets. The capabilities should be spread broadly throughout all parts of the organization (rather than in silos), have proven success in prior initiatives, have evolved in response to changes in the industry, and differentiate your company from the competition.

VALUE DEVELOPMENT

Understanding existing and needed capabilities is essential for a successful Strategy Reset.

An open and sincere assessment of your current capabilities is required. In addition, you must realistically evaluate what new capabilities can be developed. This includes finding gaps that must be closed for the vision and strategies to be successfully implemented.

TACTICAL ACTION PLAN

- **Discuss and agree on the capabilities of your company.** Examples include the ability to:
  - Respond quickly to changes in your industry.
  - Help customers improve their performance.
  - Use innovative technology to differentiate your products.

24

- **Discuss and agree on the capabilities needed to successfully implement the vision and strategies that are being developed.** Examples include the expertise to:
  o Quickly scale up large projects for implementation across the organization.
  o Develop new products on a compressed timeline.
  o Market a new product in the face of tough economic conditions.
  o Conduct research and development (R&D) that leads to new products demanded by the marketplace.
- **Discuss and agree on the gaps.** There will be gaps between current capabilities and those needed to successfully implement the vision and strategies being developed. Supply a realistic assessment of your ability to close the gaps.
- **Review all the work in this area** and decide what overall conclusions can be reached and specific strategies that may be most successful.

WHY IS THIS IMPORTANT?

A gap likely exists between your current capabilities and those needed for a successful Vision & Strategy Reset. This gap must be identified and closed, or successful implementation of the new vision and strategies may fail.

FINANCIAL ANALYSIS OF VALUE CHAINS & STRATEGY ECONOMICS

OVERVIEW

The value chain financial analysis is used to understand the profitability of different segments of your existing business. This analysis is fundamental if all the company's operations are combined for financial reporting purposes.

In addition, an economic analysis of each proposed strategy should be undertaken to understand the relative attractiveness of the different options.

VALUE DEVELOPMENT

Understanding the profitability and costs for different business segments has the benefit of supplying information about where profits are actually generated, improves management focus, results in better allocation of capital, and allows personnel to be directed toward those segments of the business that create the most value.

This financial analysis should be completed for each operating division, including the allocation of support service costs such as legal, financial, tax, and corporate management.

Economic analysis should also be completed for each strategy that involves an increase in costs or requires a capital investment.

TACTICAL ACTION PLAN

- **Generate a profit and loss (P&L) for each operating division and for support services.** Allocate the cost of support services between the operating divisions based on utilization. Are all the operating divisions profitable, or at least cash flow breakeven in a down market? Do any of the divisions experience a significant loss?

- **Calculate the economics for each proposed strategy.** This does not apply to changing operating practices or other incremental improvements that can be completed today within the existing budget. The economic analysis should include the following:

  o Internal rate of return with a fifteen-year life
  o Net present value with a fifteen-year life and five percent discount factor
  o Discounted payback period with a five percent discount factor
  o No residual value at the end of the fifteen-year life (unless new property, plant, or equipment was purchased)

  By calculating the economics for each strategy, you will be able to build up pro forma financial statements for the business with a mix of new strategies.

- **Review all the work in this area** and decide what overall conclusions can be reached and specific strategies that may be most successful.

WHY IS THIS IMPORTANT?

An economic analysis of each strategy is needed so you can quantitatively rank the potential options and decide which will achieve the financial goals you have set. Put those to the side that do not materially impact earnings levels.

Understanding the profitability of all business segments is required to focus on new strategies where profits are generated. This may be in an entirely new business line rather than through existing operations.

GOALS

Your company must set goals for the project to ensure the scope of work will accomplish everyone's objectives.

These goals will be considered as you navigate your way through each section of the work plan.

Some questions you might consider when setting the goals for the project are:

- What are the high-level objectives for this initiative?
- What would be a success story?
- What would be a disappointment?
- Why undertake the Strategy Reset at this time?
- What, if any, apprehensions are there about this initiative?

Achievement of your goals is dependent upon the engagement of everyone. Success comes from team interaction and individual ownership.

TACTICAL ACTION PLAN

The following is an example of the types of goals you might consider when developing the specific goals for your Vision & Strategy Reset.

The company has supplied the following guidance concerning the goals for the project. This was done to ensure the scope of work will accomplish the goals of the shareholders as well as the company's management team. The following should be considered as you navigate your way through each section of the work plan:

- **What are your goals for this initiative?**
  - Grow the company's earnings to achieve the following earnings before interest, taxes, depreciation, and amortization (EBITDA):

2024 - $___M EBITDA
2025 - $___M EBITDA
2026 - $___M EBITDA

- o Can you achieve the company's earnings targets using only organic growth?
- o Are the earnings targets achievable with other strategies? What are they?
- o Develop options that will allow the company to significantly increase earnings over the next two to five years.
- o Look at the management team. Does the team have the expertise needed to increase earnings levels and achieve the targets in the five-year plan?
- o Develop clear roles and responsibilities for the management team and associated decision rights.

- **What would be a success story?**

  - o Success means generating _____ EBITDA in the next three years.
  - o Success means having a unified vision and actionable strategies to significantly increase earnings over the next two to five years.
  - o Success will be having a clear understanding of our capabilities and competencies and how they relate to improving the company's profitability.
  - o Success will include reassurance that the management team has the expertise, buy-in, and proper incentives to execute the five-year plan.

- **What would be a disappointment?**

  - o Disappointment is not achieving the EBITDA stated above.

- **Why undertake the Strategy Reset at this time?**

  - o The company has a solid value proposition with our existing business. However, new strategies are needed to step up EBITDA growth.

- o The company is under pressure from new competitors and is losing market share.
- o The existing vision and strategies are no longer delivering acceptable results.

- **What, if any, apprehensions do you have about this initiative?**

  - o Will the Strategy Reset realistically allow the company to significantly increase earnings?
  - o Will we devote the necessary time to the Vision & Strategy Reset process?
  - o Will key leadership be able to work effectively as a team to achieve the goals?

WHY IS THIS IMPORTANT?

Setting clear goals will help you select the Vision & Strategy options that will deliver the most substantial results.

CASE STUDIES

The following case studies are included to give you an idea of what a successful Vision & Strategy Reset is like.

This perspective will help you craft a new Vision & Strategy for your company.

- Conoco Lubricants: Division of Conoco Inc.
- Clark Refining and Marketing, Inc.
- Flint Hills Resources, LLC: Subsidiary of Koch Industries, Inc.
- Greater Wichita YMCA
- Advance Catastrophe Technologies, Inc.
- New Technology Startup: Confidential
- Personey M&A Advisory: Owned by the author

Conoco Lubricants:
Division of a Fortune 500 Company

Conoco's lubricants division had marginal profitability, average product quality, inefficient operations, and high-cost base oil supply when I joined the group.

Problems existed in the entire value chain, starting with base oil production through packaging and distributing the finished lubricants.

Our first action was to build a model of the entire blending and packaging system, which allowed us to see the cost of the finished products delivered to customers from every supply source. Nothing like this existed in Conoco at the time.

From this model, it became clear we needed to drive down the cost of our finished products delivered to the customer. We attacked this problem in the following ways:

> ➢ Some of the blending and packaging facilities were more cost-effective than others. With this information, we closed one in-house facility, built another one closer to our customer base, closed some contract packagers, and expanded the volume blended by others. These changes dramatically reduced our finished lubricant production costs.

> ➢ The cost of lubricant additives and packaging materials was reduced by requiring suppliers to bid on the contracts. Something as simple as this resulted in significant savings.

> ➢ The distribution network was revamped to send products from whichever facility could deliver to the customer at the lowest overall cost. This change significantly improved margins.

This left the problem of what to do about average product quality that was not keeping up with changes in the marketplace and high-cost base oil supply. We reset the vision for sourcing base oil feedstock supply to address this.

The final Vision & Strategy Reset was to "Build World-Scale Production Capacity," which relied on Conoco's strength in petroleum refining. This was realized by:

> ➢ Constructing a new type of base oil manufacturing unit (lubricant hydrocracker) that produced superior products from low-cost crude oil
> ➢ Forming a joint venture with Pennzoil to achieve world-scale size and lower production costs. The Excel Paralubes joint venture was expected to be a first-quartile facility
> ➢ Shutting down uncompetitive base oil manufacturing units (Conoco) and uncompetitive refineries (Pennzoil)

The result was a complete turnaround in the lubricants division's profitability due to much lower operating costs, lower base oil costs, and a significant improvement in product quality. The strategy was unique and difficult for competitors to duplicate because:

> ➢ A large capital investment was needed to build a world-scale base oil lubricant hydrocracker facility. This cost was well beyond what most independent refining companies could manage.
> ➢ The new hydrocracking unit was designed around state-of-the-art technology, which required an extensive level of refining expertise to build and operate. This precluded most of the independent oil companies.
> ➢ The hydrocracking technology allowed the use of low-cost raw materials (feedstocks) derived from heavy sour crude oil. This ruled out all the refineries (majors and independents) that ran more expensive light crude oil.
> ➢ Conoco and Pennzoil had small, inefficient base oil units that could be shut down to supply initial product demand. This was not the case for most major oil companies.

Clark Refining and Marketing, Inc:
Owned by Private Equity

Clark had marginal profitability, small uncompetitive refineries, and was just emerging from bankruptcy when I joined the company.

Refining margins were at an all-time low, no new refining capacity was being built, uncompetitive refineries were being shut down, and the major oil companies were selling refineries.

The first thing I did was undertake the development of a model that would project the expected profitability for every refinery in the United States. It was built around a linear program using publicly available information.

The development of the model was an enormous success. It allowed us to screen all available acquisition targets against the universe of competitors in the industry to identify the facilities with a first and second-quartile competitive position.

The model was called the "Prism System," and, at the time, nothing like it was available in the US refining industry or from refining consultants.

The results of the model made it clear that radical change was required for the company to survive in the long term. The existing refineries were simply not competitive. Equally important, the Prism System also helped identify which refineries might be good acquisition candidates.

The first thing we did was optimize our existing refineries so the company could operate at cash flow breakeven, even under the worst market conditions.

This was done by tapping into the latent knowledge of employees concerning how to improve the current operations. With our employees' ideas and help, we materially improved cash flow despite a very difficult business environment.

This left the problem of how to upgrade our refinery assets. To address this, we reset the vision by moving away from an operating company mentality and taking advantage of the M&A capability brought to the company by new owners and officers. With this new capability, we transformed into a growth company.

The final Vision & Strategy Reset was to "Survive and Acquire." This was realized by:

> ➤ Recognizing that margins could not stay at current levels for an extended period; as demand grew and capacity was rationalized, margins would recover
> ➤ Recognizing that some of the majors were not running their facilities to maximize profitability (sub-optimizing their plants and incurring higher costs than needed)
> ➤ Using the Prism System to identify potential acquisition candidates, we were looking for refineries that screened well but had poor earnings as operated by the current owner

This offered an opportunity to acquire refineries that were being sold by the majors at deep discounts and improve their operations.

The Chevron Port Arthur refinery was identified this way; purchased for $76 million plus inventory, quickly turned around, and was valued at $2–3 billion within several years.

This acquisition resulted in a complete reversal of Clark's profitability and prospects. The strategy was unique and difficult for competitors to duplicate because:

> ➤ It required a point of view that refining margins would improve in three to five years. The majors did not believe this because margins had been at historic lows for several years and the independents were afraid to take the risk.
> ➤ Clark's existing refineries could be shut down or sold without a material loss of earnings because of their poor competitive position. This option was not available to other potential purchasers.

- ➢ Clark was running at cash flow breakeven to survive until margins improved. This required tapping into the latent knowledge of all employees concerning what changes could be made and having the organizational will to follow it through.
- ➢ The Port Arthur refinery had negative cash flow and needed to make significant changes. The majors were unwilling to take the risk, and the independents lacked the skills needed to recognize what was required.

Flint Hills Resources, LLC:
Subsidiary of Koch Industries, Inc.

The company had strong refining assets, favorable geographic locations, and reasonable profitability despite significant pressure on refining margins when I joined the company.

Refining margins remained at an all-time low, no new refining capacity was being built, uncompetitive refineries were being shut down, and many of the best refining assets in the United States had already come to market and had been sold.

The first thing we did was optimize the existing refineries so the company could justify new M&A growth.

This was a companywide effort focused on improving profitability and was referred to as the "Call to Action."

With ideas and help from employees across the company, we were able to materially improve earnings, which set the stage for significant capital investment in our existing refineries as well as new M&A activity.

This left the problem of where to focus our acquisitions. To address this, we reset the entire vision of the company by moving away from a pure refining platform and transforming into a diversified refining, chemicals, and biofuels company.

The final Vision & Strategy Reset was to "Acquire New Business Platforms." This was realized by:

- Purchasing other types of heavy manufacturing facilities that were experiencing depressed margins and that FHR could run with their refining capability
- Focusing on buying chemical manufacturing facilities that had depressed prices and ethanol plants with competitive advantages
- Acquiring Huntsman's Base Chemicals and Polymers business for $770 million (public filing) and materially improving the operation (the ethylene part of the

business was sold in 2020, but the purchase price was not disclosed)

This strategy resulted in substantial growth in the company's profitability and capability. This strategy was unique and difficult for competitors to duplicate because:

> ➤ Huntsman's Olefin Cracker, located in Port Arthur, Texas, had experienced a major fire and was being repaired while the sale process was underway. This was too much risk for the management of major oil companies, as well as too much risk for independent oil companies because failure of the repair project could jeopardize their entire company. After a thorough evaluation, we concluded the repair project was well run and included startup requirements in the Asset Purchase Agreement to help mitigate the risk.
> ➤ Flint Hills Resources continued making changes to improve the existing refining operations and reduce costs while at the same time absorbing the new acquisitions. This required tapping into the latent knowledge of all employees, including those who came with the acquisitions.
> ➤ Flint Hills Resources was uniquely positioned to accomplish this due to its Market-Based Management capability, which is a part of all Koch Industries companies.

Greater Wichita YMCA: Nonprofit

This nonprofit company had high-quality facilities and stable profitability when I started my advisory engagement.

However, increased competitive pressure was coming from low-cost providers and digital exercise platforms. Also, there was a high turnover of first-time members who didn't feel connected or use the facilities on a routine basis.

Building more facilities—the existing strategy—did not address these concerns.

The YMCA offers a broad range of activities, such as exercise classes, swimming, basketball, nutrition classes, youth sports, SilverSneakers, weightlifting, and martial arts, all of which have talented instructors.

The best way to address these concerns and take advantage of the YMCA's unique strengths was to reset the vision of the company.

The final Vision & Strategy Reset was to "Build Community." This was realized by:

> ➤ Creating a <u>digital</u> community to reach people who will not go to the brick-and-mortar facilities but would like to access the content and increase the retention of new members.
> ➤ Offering existing members access to the new digital programming.

The reset strategy received enthusiastic support from the local business community and other YMCA franchises.

The strategy was introduced to the public as "YMCA 360" just before the pandemic and has been a remarkable success. This strategy was unique and difficult for competitors to duplicate because:

- ➤ The digital platform includes many of the YMCA's extremely broad and diverse offerings. No other competitors can offer a similar range of activities.
- ➤ The platform includes the YMCA's high-quality influencers, many of whom are well-known. This ensures an immediate member following for the digital offerings and strong future growth in users.
- ➤ Content on the site is being contributed by YMCA organizations from across the United States. Worldwide the YMCA serves forty-five million people and is found in 10,000 communities in the United States. No other competitor comes close to matching this breadth of potential digital content or market access.

Advance Catastrophe Technologies: Privately Held

This company had stable profitability but limited earnings growth potential when I started my advisory engagement.

The strength of Advance Catastrophe Technologies (ACT) was disaster recovery in the hospitality business (e.g., hotels), a narrow subset of the entire disaster recovery industry.

They also did not have many brick-and-mortar offices spread across the United States.

The best way to address these concerns and take advantage of ACT's unique strengths was to reset the vision of the company.

The final Vision & Strategy Reset was to "Create Value for the Customer." This was realized by:

➢ Deploying mobile Critical Response Units (CRUs) where they are needed most, rather than relying on brick-and-mortar offices. The CRUs can be moved to the most profitable geographic regions or quickly shifted to areas with an ongoing disaster emergency, such as a hurricane, record low temperatures, or wildfires.

➢ Leading the adoption of new disaster recovery technology to improve the customers' experience.

➢ Introducing new client-focused services such as insurance support.

➢ Penetrating new markets by creating focused value propositions for the customer, supported by internal champions.

Implementing these strategies materially improved profitability and created significant growth potential. This strategy was unique and difficult for competitors to duplicate because:

➢ The larger competitors are heavily invested in brick-and-mortar locations that lock them into high-cost office space and specific geographic regions. In contrast, ACT's

CRUs are mobile. They can be moved to the most profitable geographic regions or quickly shifted to areas with an ongoing disaster emergency to better serve their customers.

➤ The first mover in the use of innovative technology will command customer loyalty. This requires an ongoing entrepreneurial focus, which is difficult for many companies to sustain, and that ACT has undertaken.

➤ Regional focus is the predominant business model for most companies in the disaster recovery industry. Instead, ACT will use vertical champions to bring expertise to target nationwide segments of the market. Customers value this added experience.

New Technology Startup: Confidential

This privately held company had a stable business model but limited upside potential when I started my advisory engagement.

The company's strengths were its low operating costs and established relationships in its industry.

Competitors viewed them as a niche provider of a narrow range of services. However, they also had a very innovative idea for a new product line that was not available in the market.

The best way to address these concerns and take advantage of the company's unique strengths was to reset the vision of the company.

The final Vision & Strategy Reset was realized by:

> ➢ Developing an entirely new type of product that has the potential to disrupt the entire industry. The new product would be complementary to the existing product line.
> ➢ Offering advisory services using data from the new device for an added charge.
> ➢ Penetrating the market by initially rolling out the product in the local region and then rapidly expanding from there.

Implementing these strategies is underway and is expected to result in significant upside in profitability. This strategy is unique and difficult for competitors to duplicate because:

> ➢ The new product is materially less expensive than its competitors' offerings. This opens a whole new market of smaller customers who previously did not have access to this level of expertise.
> ➢ The new product may also be attractive to larger customers because existing suppliers cannot match the prices offered by the company and remain profitable.
> ➢ This technology is entirely new, with a significant development cycle.

> ➤ The company has an advantage that will help them lock in customers by being the first to market this innovative technology.

Personey M&A Advisory:
Owned by the Author

This was a startup advisory company focused on helping companies with vision, strategy, and M&A activities.

The business was founded on three new concepts developed over forty years of professional experience. All the advisory work is based on these guiding principles:

- ➤ Vision & Strategy should be the starting point for all M&A activity, including acquisitions, divestitures, mergers, and joint ventures.
- ➤ When using M&A Best Practices, it is possible to reset the Vision & Strategy of a company, identify and complete the most attractive transactions, and generate exceptional results.
- ➤ Building your firm's vision, strategy, and M&A capability will create long-term value.

This Vision & Strategy is unique and difficult for competitors to duplicate because:

- ➤ The founder has unique experience, knowledge, and skills that allow them to recognize and utilize proven M&A Best Practices in their advisory work.
- ➤ The capability needed to offer vision, strategy, and M&A advisory rarely exists in the same person.
- ➤ Other advisors may prefer to charge significant fees for their services rather than teach their clients how to do the work. Their fees can be as high as six percent of an M&A transaction. This is not in the best interests of their clients.

LONG-TERM, FACT-BASED, STRATEGIC THINKING

The success of your current business may have resulted from several factors, including:

- Working extremely hard
- Weak competitors
- Good timing
- Outright luck

All of this is helpful, but it is different from the large amount of potential value that can be created by engaging in long-term, fact-based, strategic thinking.

The great news is you now have the tools to envision what your business can become and develop realistic strategies to make it happen.

Chapter 5
Transaction Best Practices

Transaction Best Practices are fact-based, focused, and use emotional intelligence.

They have been shown to deliver superior M&A results and are presented in the form of a success wheel with four primary elements:

Vision & Target Screening

- Everything Begins with Vision
- Why Reset Your Vision & Strategy as the First Step?
- Target Identification
- Evaluate the Competitive Position of Your Target
- Understand If the Target Has Sustainable Competitive Advantages
- Is the Transaction Actionable?
- Target Screening and Economics

Diligence Focus & Deal Team Dynamics

- Deal Team
- Diligence Preparation
- Tools for Diligence Analysis
- Key Concerns

- Focus Your Diligence
- Require Ownership

Upfront Agreement & Negotiation Style

- Upfront Agreement
- Negotiation Style Can Be Your Advantage or Your Downfall

Build M&A Capability in Your Firm

- Lead the Transaction with Your Own Team
- Pay Attention to Transition and Integration
- Act On Capturing the Economic Bets

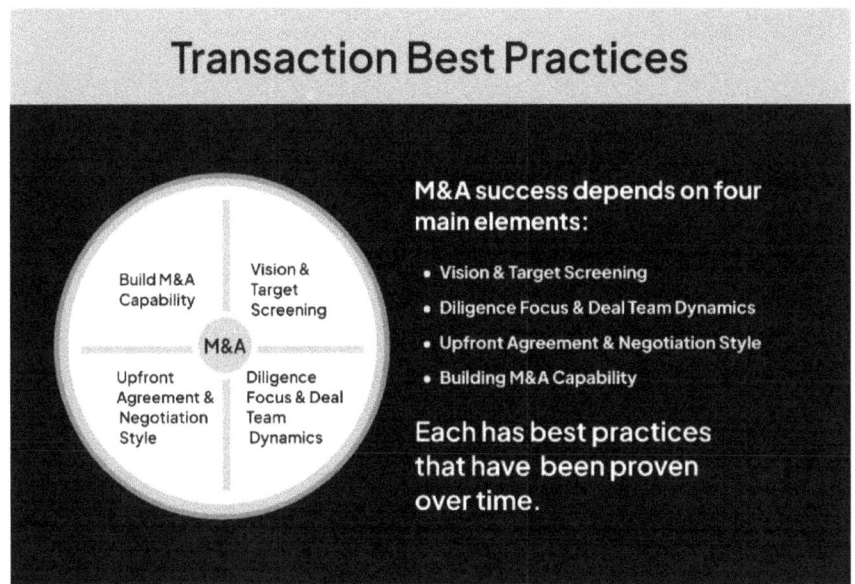

Why are these elements called transaction best practices?

Because that is what they are, as opposed to "transaction worst practices," which is, unfortunately, what many companies actually do.

To help highlight the difference, let's first compare and contrast how companies might act when using best and worst practices.

Vision & Strategy

- Worst Practice: Our current business plan is working just fine. Protect the status quo and don't rock the boat.
- Best Practice: The company has a forward looking vision with actionable strategies.

Target Screening

- Worst Practice: React to whatever comes on the market and use optimistic assumptions. "Adjust" the economics as needed to help sell the transaction.
- Best Practice: Screen transaction targets with conservative assumptions and qualitative tools to select the best targets.

Due Diligence

- Worst Practice: Use generic checklists and try to complete due diligence on everything (which is impossible).
- Best Practice: Focus your diligence on the ten to fifteen things that truly matter.

Deal Team Dynamics

- Worst Practice: The M&A lead, business owner, and a couple of attorneys do the deal with limited input and no ownership from others in the organization.
- Best Practice: The deal team will include all business areas and require ownership.

Agreement Drafting

- Worst Practice: Exchange and mark up drafts of binding legal contracts from the start.
- Best Practice: Use a term sheet to reach an agreement on key terms as the first step.

Negotiation Style

- Worst Practice: Take unreasonable positions and try to negotiate to a central point. Bluff and posture to influence the other party.
- Best Practice: Take reasonable positions, be honest and direct, and listen carefully.

M&A Capability

- Worst Practice: Hire a buy side or sell side advisor to run the transaction and only pay them if it closes.
- Best Practice: If you intend to do multiple transactions, lead the deal with your team to build your firm's M&A capability. This can be accomplished to a large extent by using your existing personnel.

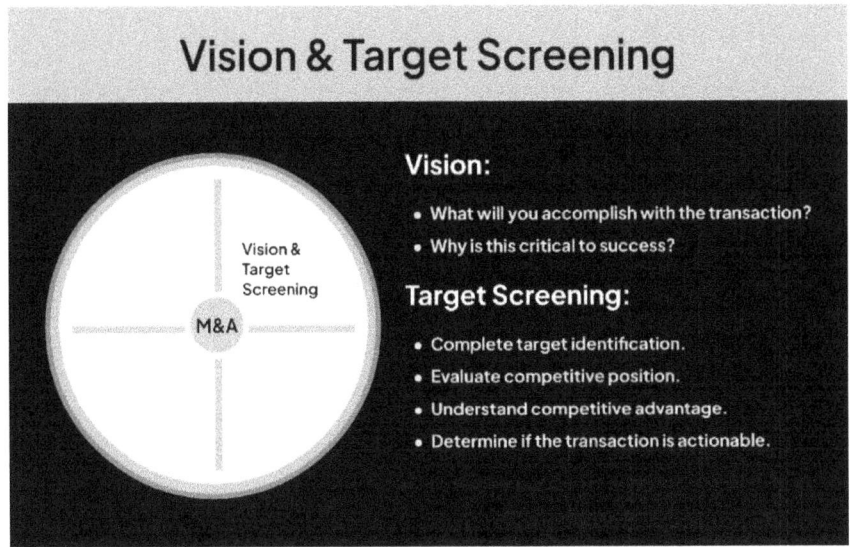

Everything Begins with Vision

Otherwise, any M&A transaction can look attractive.

Forward-looking vision, introspection, and strategy development are necessary for a successful transaction.

Many companies skip this step and go off the rails from the beginning.

Everything starts with developing a vision and actionable strategies. Without this, potentially, any transaction will look attractive.

The Strategy Reset process was covered in Chapter 4. Refer to it now if you have questions about developing a dynamic new vision with actionable strategies.

Also, if your company has not considered why they are undertaking the transaction, don't go any further until you have defined the objective and determined if it is consistent with your vision and strategies.

Why Reset Your Vision & Strategy as the First Step?

Ensure Your M&A Transactions Will Deliver Exceptional Results

Let's say your business earnings are stable, but growth is slow, and you're considering several acquisitions, but you do not realize that certain factors will negatively impact your success. Completing a Vision & Strategy Reset as the first step would help clarify all of this.

The following are examples of unexpected factors that could materially impact your transaction, along with the Strategy Reset work module (shown in parenthesis) that would make it apparent.

- A major customer is about to switch to an entirely different process and will not need your products going forward. This would be a particularly troubling time to be doubling down on the existing business model.

    (Competitor and Market Analysis)

- New disruptive technologies are about to turn the industry upside down.

    (Long-Term Macro Perspectives)

- Government initiatives are about to make it much easier for new competitors to enter your industry.

    (Long-Term Macro Perspectives)

- A different company is under financial pressure, and it would make a much more attractive acquisition target because of its synergy value.

    (Acquisition Target Identification)

- A new company is actively going after the niche market served by the acquisition target. This will reduce the target's future earnings and create the risk of overpaying.

    (Competitor and Market Analysis)

- One of several unexpected events could cause the acquisition economics to become significantly negative, thereby increasing the risk of shutdown.

(Black Swan Events)

- You make the majority of your profits in an entirely different value chain but do not realize this.

(Financial Analysis of Value Chains)

- Your acquisition economics are much lower than your organic growth options.

(Strategy Economics)

- Your company cannot successfully absorb and integrate a large acquisition, which increases the chance of a failed transaction.

(Capability Analysis)

The same is true for divestiture.

- You sell the business before making easy improvements that would improve cash flow. As a result, your sale price is too low, and the benefits from these improvements will go to the purchaser.

(Optimize Your Existing Business)

- The business is purchased by a company, which flips it to another purchaser in a short period of time for a substantial profit.

(Build M&A Capability in Your Firm)

- Your price expectations are too high, and the business is held too long. The market changes, and purchasers disappear over time.

(Long-Term Macro Perspectives)

These are just a few examples of the kinds of issues that will become apparent as part of a Vision & Strategy Reset, which could materially affect the success of a transaction.

Assuming you have completed a Vision & Strategy Reset and you are ready to consider an M&A transaction, there are four initial questions you should ask at the very beginning:

- What are you hoping to accomplish, and why is this critical to the success of your current business? If the transaction does not materially enhance your business, consider that every transaction comes with risk, which should be weighed against the potential benefits.
- How will this improve your competitive position? If the benefit is not clear, beware. A successful transaction should significantly improve your competitive position. Otherwise, it will damage the business through diluted earnings and management distraction.
- Will the transaction contribute to significant earnings growth? If you are unsure, complete more diligence until you are certain. A successful transaction should contribute significant earnings growth. If not, why are you considering it?
- Does the transaction have a reasonable risk profile? Be incredibly careful with transactions in an entirely new industry involving fourth-quartile companies or requiring significant improvements over the current operation to achieve acceptable economics. These are all elevated risk propositions. In my experience, you should avoid fourth-quartile assets or companies altogether because they will likely become shutdown candidates.
- Are you potentially leaving money on the table? A material number of transactions are flipped by the new owner for a significant gain within a brief period after closing. This money could have been captured in the first transaction with a more thorough and robust M&A process.

Let's use Clark Refining and Marketing as an example of developing a successful Vision & Strategy. At the time, I was the VP of Refining Business Development and Strategy.

In 1993 the company had two small, uncompetitive refineries, and the entire industry was struggling with depressed margins. It was difficult for many companies, including Clark and most of the majors, to operate at a profit. However, as the majors downsized their refining portfolios and merged to reduce costs, competitive refineries were coming on the market with deeply discounted prices. During this time, it was possible for refineries to be purchased at ten percent of their new replacement cost.

It was also clear that the situation could not last forever because smaller inefficient refineries had already started to shut down, and the larger players were delaying expansions due to poor economics, both of which would bring supply and demand back in balance over time. When this occurred, we expected refining margins would return to normal levels.

Considering all of this, we developed a Vision & Strategy to acquire competitive refineries with superior opportunities for improvement at deeply discounted prices while improving the performance of our existing refineries so they would operate with breakeven or positive cash flow as long as possible.

When implemented, this Vision & Strategy accomplished everything discussed above:

- Our competitive position was dramatically enhanced by adding strong new refining assets and improving the operation of what we already had.
- This resulted in significant earnings growth.
- There was minimal risk because we were buying high-quality assets.
- No money was left on the table because sale prices were severely discounted, and there were few purchasers.

The overall result was to turn the company around and change it from a shutdown candidate to an attractive ongoing concern.

Another example of developing a successful Vision & Strategy was accomplished by Conoco's lubricants division beginning in 1989. At the time, I was the Manager of Optimization.

The lubricants division held uncompetitive base oil manufacturing facilities, high-cost finished lubricant blending facilities, a web of contract blending and packaging plants that were not optimized in the supply chain, raw material suppliers that were not competing for the business (additives/packaging) and finished lubricant containers that were no longer in demand (fiber cans).

To top it all off, the market was demanding ever greater lubricant performance specifications, which made it more difficult to meet the customer's requirements unless a large amount of expensive additives were included in the blend. This was driving up costs and putting further pressure on margins. The division struggled to be profitable under these conditions and needed radical change.

The Vision & Strategy we developed was to:

- Take advantage of Conoco's refining expertise to build a new world-scale lubricant hydrocracker that could manufacture base oil that had superior performance characteristics (Group II hydrocracked base oil).
- Convert the motor oil packaging from fiber cans to rectangular plastic bottles.
- Drive down the cost of finished products by requiring suppliers to bid on the contracts for additives, packaging materials, and contract blending.
- Construct new highly efficient lubricant blending facilities that focus on supplying bulk truckloads of those lubricants that were in the highest demand.
- Optimize the existing supply network by sourcing finished products from the most cost-effective supply locations and shutting down those facilities that were uncompetitive.

Our primary concern was that we did not have sufficient internal demand for all the base oil that would be produced from the new hydrocracker facility, so we needed a partner.

After carefully looking at all the potential joint venture candidates, we decided to approach Pennzoil. They had a strong requirement for hydrocracked base oils for use in their motor oil brand. At that time, their hydrocracked base oil was being purchased from other suppliers and manufactured in their small refineries. This was a perfect match. Conoco would have the option to replace inefficient solvent extraction base oil facilities, and Pennzoil would have the option to replace small, uncompetitive refineries.

The companies formed a joint venture called Excel Paralubes, located adjacent to Conoco's Lake Charles Refinery. This new facility became one of the most competitive base oil manufacturing plants in the industry. This is an example of how to use a joint venture to "acquire" a competitive new business.

The vision and strategies for each situation will be different, but in all cases, it should help guide you toward transactions that:

- Improve your competitive position
- Contribute strongly to earnings
- Do not leave money on the table
- Have a reasonable risk profile
- Create business optionality
- Are unique and difficult for your competitors to duplicate

If a transaction does not accomplish these things, why do it?

Target Identification

Carefully Identify Your Targets—Not All Options Are Equal

Just because something is for sale, or you have been approached to form a joint venture does not mean it is your best choice. You should consider all the alternatives in the target space before deciding how to proceed.

It is often best to pass on the current opportunity if there are likely to be more attractive options available. Sometimes the best acquisitions are the ones you don't make.

- **For a purchase**, you should screen all potential acquisition targets to identify the best choice. Often a company or asset is being sold because it is disadvantaged in some way. Before continuing, you should understand this situation and have a clear plan for overcoming the shortcomings.
- **For a joint venture**, you should put together an outline of all potential interested parties and consider the advantages/disadvantages of each before deciding on a partner.
- **For a sale**, you should put together a list of all potential purchasers, both foreign and domestic, then contact all of them to determine their interest. Look at suppliers, competitors, as well as customers and include anyone interested in the sale.

Evaluate the Competitive Position of Your Target

Run from a Fourth-Quartile Company

Understanding the competitive position of a business or asset is necessary to understand the target's strength.

There are several ways to evaluate a competitive position. One of the best is the cost of production.

When this analysis includes all the competitors in an industry, it is possible to produce a "cost stack," a graph showing production capacity along the x-axis and the cost to produce along the y-axis. The strongest competitive position is indicated by the lowest cost to produce on the left side of the graph (first quartile). Conversely, the weakest competitive position is shown by the highest cost to produce on the right side of the graph (fourth quartile).

Targets in a fourth-quartile competitive position are likely to struggle with positive cash flow and should be avoided unless you have a credible plan for radical transformation. Even then, this is an elevated risk proposition. A low purchase price is meaningless if the business becomes an expensive shutdown candidate. You are better off targeting a company or asset in a first or second-quartile competitive position.

It is also possible to do competitive analysis using qualitative factors. This should be undertaken to supplement the cost stack analysis or as a separate exercise if production costs cannot be estimated.

To complete a qualitative analysis, start by finding those factors that make a business successful in a particular industry and rank each competitor by their strength. For example, for a specific industry, the most successful businesses—as evidenced by strong earnings—may have the following characteristics: feedstock advantage; high manufacturing complexity that results in more valuable products; intellectual property that is not subject to duplication; geographic advantage associated with finished product sales; large market share; and a strong management team.

The list of factors can be anything and are unique for each industry. Though not as precise as a cost stack, such an analysis can still be eye-opening if it is approached with a desire to understand the true state of affairs (as opposed to building a case for the favorite candidate).

An example of developing a successful competitive screening tool was accomplished at Clark Refining and Marketing beginning in 1993.

Our vision included growth through acquisition, but we had no way to understand the competitive strength of different targets, so an effort was undertaken to develop a model that would calculate the cost of production and project the expected profitability for every refinery in the United States. It was built around a linear program using publicly available information.

The development of the model was an enormous success. It allowed us to screen all available acquisition targets against the universe of competitors in the industry to identify the facilities with a first and second-quartile competitive position.

This led us to the Chevron Port Arthur refinery, which had projected results in this range and was on the market. However, to our surprise, the actual performance of the refinery was significantly below what we expected.

During diligence, we confirmed that the causes of the refinery's underperformance could be resolved when we gained control, so the acquisition moved forward, and this became the flagship facility for Clark and a prime asset for future owners.

The screening model developed by Clark's leadership team was so innovative that it is still being used by the refining industry today. Similar concepts could be applied to any industry.

Understanding If the Target Has Sustainable Competitive Advantages

A Competitive Advantage May Erode Over Time

It is equally important to understand if your target's competitive advantages are sustainable or if they are likely to erode over time.

- Real value comes from advantages that are unlikely to change. Examples might be advantaged geographic location, feedstock supply, technology, market access, and industry barriers to entry.

  However, an advantage will be eroded over time if it is subject to competitive pressure. Your competitors will find a way to take away this advantage.

- You should also consider societal changes that may affect a business, such as a potential new source of energy, breakthrough battery technology, aging of the population, expansion of overseas competitors, or the chance of a recession. Often, these factors can have a greater impact on the long-term success of a business than anything else.

For example, I took part in a transaction that depended upon a low crude oil price for the economics to be attractive. We did not consider the implications of ongoing changes in the world's geopolitical situation, which had the potential to cause a significant rise in prices.

Unfortunately, this is exactly what happened, which caused lower earnings during the early years of ownership with a corresponding reduction in net present value (NPV). Had we considered this possibility, it might have been possible to negotiate a lower purchase price or use an earnout where a part of the price would depend upon certain market conditions remaining in place.

A similar thing occurred before a significant recession. In retrospect, it was clear there were excesses in the financial markets. We should have considered the possibility of a recession as one of our planning scenarios so we could be positioned to take advantage of the resulting opportunities. Unfortunately, this did not happen, and the company, like many others, backed away from attractive transactions during this period.

Is the Transaction Actionable?

It Is Pointless to Focus On Targets That Are Unlikely to Be in Play

When you have completed your competitive analysis and identified attractive targets, the next consideration is actionability.

- Extremely competitive companies and assets (first quartile) are rarely offered for sale at realistic prices unless it is the result of a merger. In other words, they are not actionable. You should move on to consideration of other targets but react quickly if they ever come to the market.
- However, these same companies and assets could make excellent joint venture partners because of their strength. To attract their interest, you will need to bring

true value and synergy to the venture. Without significant value creation, they are not actionable as a venture partner.

- The sales process is different. In this case, you should approach all potential candidates using a teaser and let them tell you if they are interested. A purchaser can come from anywhere.

On occasion, I have been asked to complete detailed screening analyses on potential targets that were clearly not actionable. This always turned out to be a waste of time.

Unless you have a lot of surplus resources, only focus on actionable targets.

Target Screening and Economics

Look for a Home Run; Pass On Everything Else

The primary factor when screening transaction targets is to decide if they have the potential to create significant economic value (a home run). This may seem obvious, but getting caught up in "deal frenzy" and pursuing a marginal target can easily happen.

The following are some of the metrics you should consider when screening your targets:

- **Net present value/internal rate of return (NPV/IRR):** Look for an unlevered internal rate of return (IRR) more than twenty percent, a discounted payout period of one to three years, and a significant net present value (NPV). When all three conditions are present, you have a strong opportunity.

  A high internal rate of return (IRR) with a small net present value (NPV) represents a project incapable of contributing significant earnings growth and will distract focus from other higher-value activities.

An extended discounted payback period characterizes a project that is at risk of marketplace changes over time because cash flow is back-end loaded.

A significant NPV with a low IRR indicates a project that will consume valuable investment resources that may be better used on different opportunities.

- **Competitive Position:** As discussed above, you should only consider targets with a first or second-quartile competitive position.

Third-quartile candidates should also be avoided for the simple reason that they are already under competitive pressure.

Fourth-quartile targets are marginally competitive and extremely risky; the chance of shutdown is high. A low price does not mean it is a great deal; you should complete an analysis of shutdown expenses as part of your evaluation. It is not as simple as closing the door on a bad transaction. Once a business is shut down, you may have continued obligations for contracts that cannot be canceled (with take or pay provisions), rail car leases that cannot be vacated, demolition obligations, employee severance costs, environmental cleanup costs, and so on. Sometimes the shutdown cost can be many times more than your original investment.

- **Competitive Advantages:** Identify those targets with sustainable competitive advantages that are unlikely to be eroded. Such targets do not come on the market very often and should be highly valued because you have some assurance that your cash flow projections will hold up over time.

- **Other Potential Sources of Value:** Sometimes called "free option value," this can make a substantial difference in the ultimate attractiveness of a target. This includes such things as:

- o Does the target control technology with potential applications in other industries?
- o Could the transaction improve feedstock supply by securing a scarce resource?
- o Will the target benefit from ongoing and future changes in society? Examples of future changes in society could be the transition to electric vehicles, aging workforce, personalized medicine, increased use of artificial intelligence, and continued expansion of digital social connections.
- o Can you easily expand the business into entirely new industries?

All these items speak to upside potential, which may heavily favor one target over another.

- **Economic Cases:** At a minimum, you should complete the standard economic cases, including extreme downside case, base case, and upside case. Each of these has a purpose.

  The extreme downside case gives you a look at potentially how bad the economic return can be. Your target should be at least cash flow breakeven in the extreme downside case.

  The base case is your investment decision case. All bets in the base case (e.g., lower costs/improved margins) should have an owner, and you will be executing against this case.

  The upside case gives you an idea of the upside earnings potential using assumptions that are likely to occur.

  It is best to make conservative assumptions in all these cases because the chance of a downside surprise is usually greater than an unexpected upside windfall.

- **Big Picture:** You should also complete a big-picture scenario analysis. This is where you evaluate the impact of different macroeconomic scenarios on transaction economics.

These are not Black Swan events but things that can easily occur, such as an economic recession beginning at the start of the project, corporate tax rates returning to thirty-five percent, the price of oil dropping to $40 per barrel and staying there, a carbon tax put in place to pay down the national debt, and a major new pandemic.

The list of scenarios should be customized based on the targets' primary risk factors. Sometimes this analysis can be more enlightening than the initial economic cases.

- **Target's Business Options:** Another consideration is the business options available to the target. For example, suppose the company is financially secure. In that case, you will have to pay a premium, or it may not be in play, while a midsized competitor under some financial pressure may be the more attractive target.

  Pay particular attention to assets and businesses that are being divested as a result of a merger. These can be remarkably high quality with a limited number of purchasers because of high market concentration among the remaining players, which leaves an opening for an outsider to enter the industry in a strong position.

- **Do not try to steal the business:** It is highly likely you will be outbid, lose the opportunity, and create a negative impression with the seller, which could affect future opportunities. Instead, bid a fair price and avoid pressure from the seller to walk up your offer.

To give you an example of what not to do, I took part in a large transaction with a mix of strong and weak assets. Some were first-quartile performers, while others were struggling.

The decision was made to buy the entire group of assets without a complete understanding of the competitive position of each major asset or the costs involved in shutting down the underperformers.

I pushed back on this decision because the seller was willing to carve out the weak assets but was overruled by senior management, who believed the risks could be managed in a portfolio fashion.

Within a few years, the uncompetitive assets were being closed due to poor earnings. The company absorbed significant shutdown and demolition expenses that could have been avoided by excluding fourth-quartile assets from the very start.

Remember your goal should be to only target those transactions that:

- Improve your competitive position
- Contribute strongly to earnings
- Do not leave money on the table
- Have a reasonable risk profile
- Create business optionality
- Are unique and difficult for your competitors to duplicate

Diligence Focus & Deal Team Dynamics

M&A

Diligence Focus & Deal Team Dynamics

There can be hundreds of diligence items and only 10–15 that matter.

- Identify and focus your diligence on the few critical items.
- Pinpoint key bets and include them.
- Determine an owner for each diligence item and bet.

Deal team must represent all groups and have a stand-alone identity.

Setting up the deal team and focusing your diligence are two of the most significant activities in the M&A process.

When done properly, they will ensure you are not surprised by serious items that should have been discovered before the transaction is closed.

In addition, focused diligence and a strong deal team will allow you to reflect the diligence findings in the purchase agreement by negotiating a price reduction, requiring additional representations, or shifting liabilities to the seller. In some cases, it may even cause you to rethink whether you want to go forward with the transaction.

Better to discover all these things upfront before executing a binding purchase agreement.

Deal Team

Set up the Deal Team with Representatives from All Areas

The deal team should represent all major areas of the business and be involved from the start of the transaction through signing, transition, closing, and integration.

- It is important that you include all the people who will be responsible for running the business on the team. This is the best way to avoid handoff confusion and lack of ownership concerning diligence findings and economic bets.
- The deal team should be led by an M&A person responsible for the overall coordination of activities and negotiation of the transaction agreements. Co-leaders would include the commercial person with P&L responsibility for the new business and an M&A attorney. This way, all diligence findings will be reflected in the agreements, and the commercial lead will be fully aware of all material matters.
- Before the process is complete, every deal team member should be responsible for some part of the diligence and/or the economic bets being made. If someone is uncomfortable with this commitment, finding an alternative person to serve on the team would be best.
- Set up a standing deal team meeting at least once a week to keep everyone connected and reinforce communication.

  The purpose of this meeting is not to report on the status of activities but to discuss areas of concern to get the group's input and make other members aware of items that may be important to them (e.g., "I ran across a reference to groundwater contamination in an unrelated document. Does anyone need this information?")

- The team's overall performance will be strongest if you can develop a sense of pride in being a team member.

There are several ways to do this, and a good start is for the chief executive officer (CEO) to ask the entire organization to support the deal team.

- Finally, the M&A leader and all deal team members must have seamless teamwork. There is no room for friction between individuals or organizational politics. Everyone is in this together.

These lessons were first learned when I led M&A transactions at Clark. We had a small organization, and everyone understood that we were all accountable. As a result, the deal team functioned seamlessly, had a high degree of camaraderie, and achieved outstanding results.

Diligence Preparation

Prepare for Diligence by Gaining Access to Detailed Information

To get ready for the due diligence process, gather as much information as you can about the counterparty and the transaction.

Beware of pushback from a seller or potential joint venture partner if they are unwilling to supply any of the following because this may be a sign of material problems:

- Detailed confidential information memorandum (CIM)
- Historical financial information prepared in accordance with generally accepted accounting principles (GAAP)
- Access to facilities
- Access to knowledgeable personnel
- Access to an electronic data room
- Complete answers to your written questions

Remember that the seller or joint venture partner knows more about the business than you do. Insist on complete and transparent disclosure.

To give you an example, I was once involved in a transaction where it was clear that the seller was not being truthful. We were also not given access to all the facilities or people needed to make informed decisions. However, senior management decided the concerns were not that great, so the decision was made to go forward with the deal.

This turned out to be a mistake. The reality was far worse than expected and resulted in unexpected downtime, substantial added capital investment, higher operating costs, lower production levels, and much lower earnings.

Any red flags that come up during diligence or any sign the counterparty is not being truthful should be cause for concern. In this situation, do yourself a favor and back away from the transaction.

Tools for Diligence Analysis

Take the Time to Complete a Thorough Diligence Analysis

There are no shortcuts for due diligence. Take the time to complete a thorough analysis using the tools listed below to help you find areas of significant concern.

- Prepare a table of all major contracts and licenses. Look for contracts that include take or pay provisions, expire in the near future, can easily be canceled by the counterparty, have consent requirements, or have change of control provisions.
- Prepare and send a risk assessment questionnaire covering corporate liabilities, compliance, and environmental risks. Look for a complete understanding of these risks as well as good corporate governance in these areas.
- Prepare a table of environmental permits showing if each permit is transferable and if consent is needed. Look for permits that are not transferable or where government consent is unlikely to be granted.
- Prepare a table of real property, including a description of the property and ownership. Look for real property that is not owned by the target but is being leased as well

as real property that is being excluded from the transaction.

- Prepare a table of pipeline right-of-way, including a description of each piece of right-of-way. Look for gaps in the right-of-way and if it is transferable.
- Prepare a table of patents, trademarks, and other intellectual property, including a description and whether it is transferable. Look for intellectual property (IP) that is not owned by the target as well as IP that is being excluded from the transaction.
- Prepare an analysis of the target's earnings to determine if it benefits from artificial support in the form of favorable legislation or sweetheart contracts, both of which are subject to change and can reduce earnings.
- Prepare an analysis of hidden liabilities that may not manifest until well into the future. This includes corporate liabilities from other legal entities that were purchased in the past, significant unresolved environmental contamination, potential product liabilities, major contract liabilities or losses that have not been recognized, such as derivatives, and pending litigation concerning intellectual property, product liability, personal injury, and contract disputes.

Key Concerns

Hundreds of Diligence Items and Only 15–20 That Truly Matter

In every transaction, only fifteen to twenty diligence items truly matter, so it is extremely easy to get lost in the hundreds of other details that will be encountered along the way. Counteract this by preparing a list of key concerns made up of fifteen to twenty items using the process outlined below.

- To help you identify and focus on the most important items, prepare by reviewing all available information from the seller. Typically, this is a confidential information memorandum (CIM), management presentation, and a data room. You are looking for red flags and information that should have been disclosed but is missing. These become the initial items on the list of key concerns.

- Now add significant items from the diligence analysis tools described above.
- In addition, you should include lessons from previous transactions. The M&A person on the deal team should take the lead in preparing an initial list of critical areas in earlier transactions.
- Also, ask each deal team member to consider the three worst things they could find during due diligence in their area and include these items as part of the list.
- This would be followed by a series of meetings with the deal team to customize the list for this particular transaction. The M&A person would lead these meetings and update the list as your diligence progresses.
- The list should only include items that can have a very material impact on the economics or success of the transaction; remove everything else.
- Finally, every key concern and every bet that is included in the economics should have an owner on the deal team who is responsible for evaluating that item and supplying feedback to the negotiating team and the economics group.

Below are a few questions you should ask when preparing your list of key concerns. You should customize the list for each transaction:

M&A

- o What is the competitive position of each major production facility within the company? Are some of the assets fourth-quartile performers?
- o Reconcile actual financial results with your economic models. Is there a gap?

- o Are new government regulations being considered that would have an impact on the target (e.g., a carbon tax)?
- o What is the effect of other macro changes in society, regulations, and the world economy on the transaction? (Look back at the analysis completed during your Strategy Reset.)

Commercial

- o Are there supply chain risks?
- o Are product specifications changing?
- o Are new competitors entering the market?
- o Does favorable legislation benefit earnings?

Operations

- o Don't buy junk. Understand asset quality and mechanical integrity.
- o What is causing unplanned downtime?
- o Why are sustaining capital expenditures high/low?
- o Impact of climate change on the assets (e.g., rising sea levels)?

Environmental

- o Are they operating within their environmental permits?
- o Is there significant environmental contamination on/off-site?
- o Can the environmental permits be transferred?

Legal

- o What major liabilities exist within the company?
- o Are there antitrust, corruption, or trade sanctions violations?
- o Do they have any significant ongoing litigation?
- o Do some major contracts include take or pay requirements?
- o Confirm the ownership structure of the company.

When you identify the items most significant to your transaction, the value of your diligence will dramatically improve.

Focus Your Diligence

The Key Concerns Are Most Important

After the transaction is closed and you have been running the business for a while, it will be clear what diligence items were most important. However, at that point, it is too late to change the purchase price or modify any of the agreements. Always remember the seller knows more about the business than you can ever hope to understand before closing.

To counteract this, <u>focus</u> your diligence on the areas of key concern you have identified. Include them as headline items in the overall diligence work plan and revisit them weekly during the standing deal team meetings.

The key concerns list should also be a real-time document that changes over time. As you learn more about the business, some items will come off the list when it becomes clear they are not major factors in the transaction's success, and others will be added when their critical nature is recognized.

In this way, you will always be working on what you have determined are the most important items as the transaction progresses. This also allows you to adjust the price and deal terms as the true facts become clear and before you have signed binding agreements that cannot be changed. In some cases, you may back away from the transaction entirely.

I have used this process many times with excellent results. It allowed us to stay focused on the critical factors that could affect the success of the transaction and not be distracted by the hundreds of other items that did not.

Require Ownership

Personal Ownership Will Inspire Excellent Work

Before the purchase agreements are signed, and again before the transaction is closed, each member of the deal team should be expected to give their personal "good to go" concerning the evaluation of each diligence item or economic bet they own, as well as a reflection of any concerns they have raised in the final transaction agreements.

The "good to go" should be asked for in the deal team meeting before signing the agreements and immediately before closing the transaction with no repercussions for a "no go" vote.

There is nothing like personal ownership to ensure complete focus and the best work by everyone on the team.

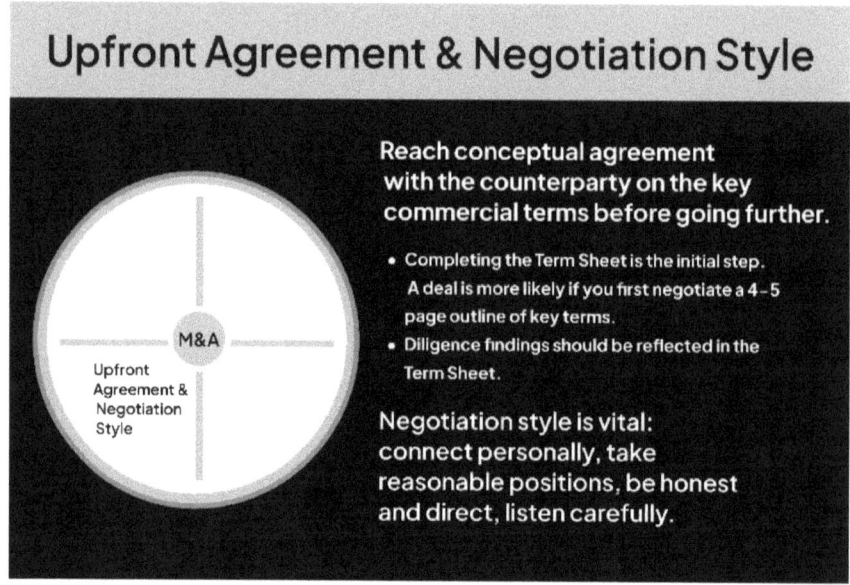

Upfront agreement and negotiation style are two areas where my recommendations differ importantly from the typical M&A practice.

Reaching an early upfront agreement with the counterparty and negotiating in a straightforward approach are both critical to achieving the best price and transaction terms.

Upfront Agreement

Increase Your Chances of Reaching a Deal with an Upfront Agreement

A deal is much more likely to succeed if you reach an upfront agreement on a detailed outline of key commercial terms as the first step.

This is a transaction-gating item. In my experience, if you cannot reach an agreement on a high-level outline of the transaction, followed by a more detailed term sheet (a four-to-five- page outline of the key commercial terms), it is unlikely that a deal will ever be reached, and there is no point in continuing discussions.

Using a term sheet also ensures that stakeholders in your company understand the deal and agree with your negotiation positions. The last thing you want is to get well down the road before discovering you do not have the necessary internal support to complete the transaction.

Finally, you can use the term sheet to keep everyone in your company informed as things change during negotiations and to ensure diligence findings are properly reflected in the terms.

Start this process by organizing your thoughts into a high-level outline of the transaction. Use this outline for your initial discussions with the counterparty to ensure everyone is on the same page concerning what the transaction will involve.

Consider asking the following questions to organize the discussion:

1) What will my company do (e.g., purchase assets)?
2) What will my company not do (e.g., assume debt or significant liability)?
3) What will the counterparty do (e.g., sell assets and inventory)?
4) What will the counterparty not do (e.g., be responsible for post-closing liabilities)?

From this very simplified example, it is apparent there may be a disconnect between the parties concerning the retention and transfer of existing liabilities, some of which may not become apparent until after closing. To resolve this, continue discussions with the counterparty until everyone can agree on a high-level outline of the transaction.

You might also want to create a visual example of the transaction to facilitate the discussion. This is called a "Transaction Flowchart." There is an example in Chapter 10: Toolbox.

After you have agreed on a high-level outline of the transaction, use this document to prepare a detailed term sheet that would then be reviewed with the counterparty.

The Documents Matter section in Chapter 9 includes a complete discussion of how to prepare a detailed term sheet for an acquisition, divestiture, and joint venture. There is also an example of an acquisition term sheet in Chapter 10: Toolbox.

Negotiation Style Can Be Your Advantage or Your Downfall

Taking Unreasonable Positions Is a Loser's Strategy

There are two different negotiation philosophies.

The typical approach is to take unreasonable positions and try to negotiate toward an acceptable middle point.

The best practice approach is to take reasonable positions and resist material concessions. This is what I strongly recommend.

The standard negotiating strategy is unlikely to yield the best results because the counterparty will question your sincerity about negotiating the deal. It also trains them to push back on every position, even when you are trying to find the middle ground.

It is ideal when a counterparty uses the standard approach. Why? Because they know their offer is unreasonable, and you are now in the driver's seat.

You can reject their offer outright, question their credibility, and challenge their interest in completing the transaction.

Now the only option they have is to chase you with an attractive new proposal, which may be much better than you would have initially requested.

In contrast, by taking reasonable positions, you force the counterparty to try and explain why your very reasonable positions are not acceptable.

This is an uncomfortable and dangerous position for them.

You are in a much stronger negotiating situation by taking reasonable positions, and you may be able to capture material concessions from the counterparty beyond what you originally thought possible.

The best deal will be achieved by connecting with the counterparty on a personal level, taking reasonable positions, and being honest and direct. Do not waste their time with posturing. One exposed lie or failed bluff will destroy your credibility, and the counterparty will not believe anything you say from that point on.

Also, listen carefully to what they say and watch their body language. Often, the counterparty will tell you how to overcome their objections by what they say at the negotiating table (assuming you have a good working relationship) or during sidebar discussions with their team members.

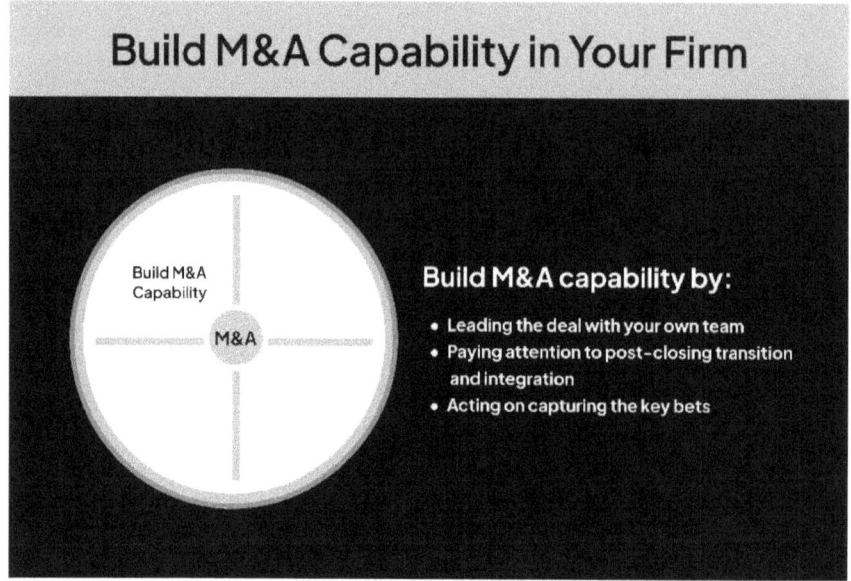

Lead the Transaction with Your Team

Avoid the Success Fee Trap

If you hire another company to lead the transaction, you will still do most of the work, pay large fees, educate them about the industry, and must hire them again for the next deal.

In addition, some of these firms are chasing success fees, which may cause them to provide advice that is not in your best interests.

There is a better way.

Instead, lead the deal with your team to build a new vision, strategy, and M&A capability in your firm that will continue to create value in the future. This can be accomplished to a large extent by using your existing personnel.

Pay Attention to Transition and Integration

Skip This Step, and You Will Put the Entire Transaction in Peril

At some point, you will have a signed agreement, and efforts will begin to close the transaction.

You should simultaneously prepare for transition and integration. Both areas are as important as negotiating the transaction but are rarely treated that way.

To stay on top of this, you should expand the due diligence work plan to include transition and integration items with owners for each item.

Approach this the same way you developed the initial list of key concerns. Ask each member of the deal team to identify the three worst things that could go wrong. These become the headline items, and you will build out the details.

This part of the due diligence work plan should also be updated in real-time as you learn more about running the business.

Now refocus the deal team on transition and integration to ensure the transaction comes out of the gate strongly.

If there are antitrust approvals involved, you must wait until those are obtained before going forward with transition and integration. When those are received, or if they are not necessary, move forward as quickly as possible.

Act On Capturing the Economic Bets

Your Long-Term Success Depends on This

Congratulations! You have closed the transaction, and integration is underway.

Can you let up now and assume that everything will be okay? What about the bets that were included in the transaction economics? They will not happen on their own.

It should have been clear throughout the diligence process which person owns each of the bets included in the transaction economics.

Now is the time to make sure the bets are met by holding these individuals accountable for achieving the expected results.

The best way to supply the necessary focus is to include the bets in each person's annual goals during the next three to five years.

Capturing the bets made in your acquisition economics will determine if the transaction is a success. However, it is easy to gloss over this effort and go back to business as usual. If you allow this to happen, the transaction is sure to underperform.

M&A Worst Practices

Common and Serious Mistakes I Have Witnessed

This discussion would not be complete without pointing out what happens when "M&A worst practices" are used. Following are some of the most common and serious mistakes you should be careful to avoid.

- **Buying fourth-quartile assets as indicated by either historical or projected earnings.** This is an extremely high-risk proposition that should never be undertaken without a realistic estimate of shutdown costs (which is likely) and a downward reduction in the purchase price.
- **"Adjusting" the economic assumptions, prices, and earnings to help sell the transaction.** This will result in unachievable earnings projections and an inflated purchase price. I am aware of several circumstances where this practice resulted in the company's bankruptcy.
- **Taking unrealistic positions during negotiations.** This is sure to destroy your credibility with the counterparty, may cost you the deal, and could force you to offer a higher price and better terms than if you had been reasonable from the start.

- **Overpaying**. This will cause the acquisition to underperform no matter what you do from that point forward.
- **Trying to steal the deal.** You will be outbid, or the sellers will decide not to move forward, and you will lose the deal.
- **Chasing every deal.** Just because something is for sale doesn't mean it is an attractive acquisition. Chasing every deal dilutes available time and resources.
- **Getting lost in diligence and missing the 10 to 15 most important items**. This can cause unexpected costs, unexpected liabilities, and underperforming earnings.
- **Not completing thorough diligence and instead relying on the reps and warranties.** This sets up future litigation, which is expensive, distracting, and has limited ability to recover all your losses.
- **Not having clear ownership of the bets made in the economics and not following through on capturing these items.** This is certain to result in an underperforming transaction; the bets will not happen alone.

Transaction Best Practices - Concluding Thoughts

This chapter focused on explaining the ideas and methods used in Transaction Best Practices.

They may be unlike anything you have experienced before and are proven to improve transaction success.

I encourage you to internalize and use this new knowledge; there is no doubt your achievements will dramatically improve.

Chapter 6
Additional Lessons

Additional lessons that are vital for your M&A success are covered in this portion of the book.

This information is valuable in certain circumstances, so you should review it in detail before beginning any transactions.

The material is grouped into the following categories:

Effective Negotiations

- Use Principles to Guide Negotiations
- Align Incentives for Success
- Sellers have Four Primary Drivers
- Face-to-Face Considerations
- Always Another Alternative

Acquisition Integration

- People are the Most Valuable Asset
- Adopt the Acquisitions Best Practices

Diagnose M&A Failures

- Understanding Failures is Essential for Long-Term Success

Business Optimization

- Optimize Underperforming Businesses Before You Begin

Questions You Should Ask When Approached to Invest

- Screen the Counterparty Upfront

All Companies Can Build M&A Capability

- The Size of Your Company is Irrelevant

Effective Negotiations

Use Principles to Guide Negotiations

Before beginning negotiations with the counterparty, reduce the transaction to broad principles and major negotiating positions.

This will help prevent transaction drift, where the counterparty maneuvers you into a much less attractive deal and will keep the transaction on track to accomplish what you intend.

For example, some transaction principles might be:

- All pre-closing environmental liabilities, both known and unknown, will remain with the seller.
- All intellectual property necessary to run the business will be transferred or licensed to the purchaser at no added cost.
- All key management personnel will remain with the business unless the purchaser decides not to hire them.

If you lay out your negotiation positions in broad principles and build them into the term sheet, it will be possible to assess and decide how to react to individual points when they arise.

Align Incentives for Success

Consider the motivations of the parties before you begin. Are incentives aligned on important matters?

For example, suppose your purchase price is based on the current performance of the business, but the seller wants a premium based on potential future improvements. This difference must be resolved, or the transaction will fail.

In this situation, an earnout may align incentives. The base purchase price would be paid at closing, but the seller could receive an added payment (earnout) after closing if earnings are stronger than expected.

A term sheet is a helpful tool because you can work through different conceptual options with the counterparty before building things out in greater detail.

You should do this for all major areas of difference and decide if they can be bridged early in the discussion.

If incentives cannot be aligned, the chance of reaching an agreement is unlikely, and you should move on to other opportunities.

Sellers Have Four Primary Drivers

Sellers have four primary concerns that drive their actions. In advance of negotiating the term sheet, consider how you can offer flexibility in these areas while simultaneously holding firm on matters that are the most important to you.

- Value Received
- Division of Liability
- Speed of Transaction
- Certainty of Closing

Your chance of transaction success will improve by addressing these concerns for the seller.

Value Received

The value received by the seller is always their first consideration. This includes acquisition price and payments made for other items, such as inventory.

Consider if you can offer a modest change in price without materially impacting your economics.

The value received can also include other items, such as transferring debt to the purchaser or taking on other liabilities. Consider what you can manage at a lower cost than the seller.

Division of Liability

Most of the time, this is related to the transfer of environmental liability from the seller to the purchaser, but it can also include product liability, litigation, and other matters.

Be careful here. Environmental and other liabilities can have open-ended costs and exceptionally long life.

Hold firm for a fair and equitable division of liability.

Speed of Transaction

The time required to negotiate the agreements, complete your diligence, and close the transaction is of concern to the seller.

This is because the more time it takes to close the transaction, the greater chance you may try to negotiate a lower purchase price or different agreement terms.

Keep in mind that the seller knows vastly more about the business than you do at this point.

As a result, I do not recommend cutting any corners when completing your due diligence or negotiating the agreements. Thorough diligence is your best protection against negative post-closing surprises.

However, it may be possible to develop a relationship with the seller before a potential transaction so you can clear some of this out of the way and move quickly when the opportunity arises.

Certainty of Closing

The more certainty of closing you can offer, the more attractive your proposal will be.

For example, the seller will find it attractive if you can offer to close the transaction without a financing contingency (third-party financing). This is because the new debtholders may require a lower purchase price and changes in the transaction agreements, all of which will slow down the process and may cause an impasse between the parties.

This is another reason to negotiate a detailed term sheet before drafting agreements. In this way, the seller will know exactly where you stand on all material matters before contract drafting begins.

The seller's worst-case scenario is a failed transaction.

If this happens, the seller must start over with a new purchaser who realizes the transaction failed and is now in a stronger negotiating position to demand both a lower price and better terms.

Face-to-Face Considerations

When negotiating face-to-face, your approach to the discussions can make the difference between success and failure.

Use the following principles to improve your transaction success:

- Understand the counterparty's primary value drivers and considerations. This will help guide all your negotiating positions.
- Develop an honest and open relationship with the primary negotiator. This is the best way to ensure you satisfactorily address their most important concerns during negotiations and have an open line of communication to find creative solutions that work for both parties.
- Talk less and listen carefully; many times, the counterparty will tell you what they will accept through their comments.
- Pay attention to sidebar conversations and body language. Sometimes this will tell you more than what they actually say during negotiations.
- Help the counterparty craft a great "story" for their internal consumption so long as your economic cost is small. The deal will die if they cannot sell it internally.

- Base your negotiating positions on hard analysis/economics. Be prepared to give up things that do not materially affect your economics but are important to the counterparty in exchange for the most important things to you.
- Effectively use screening economics to quickly assess the economic effect of different negotiating positions.
- Remain flexible in your positions and give the counterparty as many options as possible. Sometimes they will make a choice that gives you more value than their original request.
- Make extensive use of external challenge resources to review your negotiating positions. This will help prevent a "We are right, and they are obviously wrong" mentality that will get in the way of completing the deal.
- There is always more than one option. You should consider two or three alternatives to the current transaction to ensure this is the best choice. For example, a merger, joint venture, or commercial agreement could generate more value for your company rather than an acquisition.

Always Another Alternative

Be careful not to lock yourself into discussions with only one seller.

It is strongly recommended that you simultaneously consider two or three different acquisitions. This provides an alternative if you reach an impasse on one of the deals and helps ensure you are working on the transaction that generates maximum value for the company.

The same also applies in the case of a disposition. Always simultaneously negotiate with at least two counterparties so that you have an alternative if you reach an impasse with the lead purchaser.

Acquisition Integration

People Are the Most Valuable Asset

The most valuable asset in any acquisition is the people, and the biggest fear within the target company is a reduction in force.

Protect your investment in the people by:

- Communicating often and clearly about both the acquisition and transition.
- Show that you are serious about keeping key players by immediately placing them in responsible positions and announcing this as soon as the transaction closes.
- Assure key players that they are valued and that their jobs are not at risk. Consider offering select employment contracts. High-performing individuals will not put up with uncertainty and will start looking for other employment if they feel at risk.
- Have empathy for the new people and help them adjust to your work processes. This type of transition is difficult under the best circumstances. Imagine if the tables were turned. What would you want from the purchaser?

Adopt the Acquisition's Best Practices

Recognize that the acquisition's intellectual property, processes, and procedures may be superior to yours in some cases.

To ensure the value is captured:

- Make a concerted effort to learn from the newcomers and consider their ideas for integration. They know more about the acquisition company than you do and can make a valuable contribution.
- Commit to using the best practices from both companies, not just "our way."

I do not recommend forcing the acquisition to completely adopt your way of doing things or setting up the acquisition as a stand-alone division insulated from the parent company. In both cases, there is a risk you may not recognize or take advantage of the acquisition's best practices.

Diagnose M&A Failures

Understanding Failures Is Essential for Long-Term Success

If you want to improve your transaction success, swallow your pride and post-audit all your M&A transactions one year after closing and again three years after closing.

The one-year audit is to catch early problems while there is still time to make corrections.

The three-year audit takes a hard look at what worked so you can reinforce this practice and what did not work so you can adjust before the next transaction. After three years, you will have a good picture of how the transaction is performing compared to the acquisition economics.

Some of the questions you should ask at the one-year post-audit are as follows:

- Has your margin point of view developed as expected?
- Have you followed up on the economic bets that were included in your analysis? Do the results match your expectations?
- Have all the items in the transition work plan been successfully completed?
- Are initial earnings and cash flow meeting expectations?
- Did you miss any areas of key concern in your due diligence?
- Have there been negative surprises that resulted from fast-tracking the acquisition process?

Some of the questions you should ask at the three-year post-audit are as follows:

- Did your macro case scenarios fairly represent what has actually happened?
- Have there been any disagreements with the seller over the meaning of the contract language?

- Have there been unexpected positive or negative developments that have significantly affected the economics?
- Has the competitive position of the acquisition changed?
- Have you been able to capture the expected levels of synergy?
- Have you been able to implement the expected profit improvement projects?

Business Optimization

Optimize Underperforming Businesses Before You Begin

Optimizing underperforming businesses before starting any M&A transaction is an essential first step.

By improving your current cash flow, you will be in a better negotiating position, and it will help you avoid leaving money on the table by:

- o Giving you room to wait for excellent deal terms
- o Ensuring the maximum sale price is achieved
- o Making sure the best joint venture (JV) valuation is realized

Consider replacing weak assets with something entirely new that will move the business from the fourth quartile to the first quartile. This can be done with direct investment in innovative technology. It is also sometimes possible to buy a stronger asset and shut down a part of your existing operations.

If your existing business is under competitive pressure, you should look for radical transformation rather than incremental improvements. Consider how the Chinese are putting all their focus on electric cars rather than trying to make a competitive internal combustion automobile.

Tap into the knowledge of your existing employees. I have done this with four companies, and the effort yielded substantial improvements in profitability and many new initiatives. The employees already know how to improve profits, but the current environment may not offer an opportunity for them to help. Create a process for them to take part in improving the business as if they were owners, and you will be pleased with the results.

Often an independent perspective is needed to radically change the direction of an organization that is heavily invested in the status quo. Start with a cold-eye review of your business, consider resetting your Vision & Strategy, and develop creative new initiatives for radical transformation.

Questions You Should Ask When Approached to Invest

Screen the Counterparty Upfront

When you are approached to invest in a potential transaction, you should ask the following questions to screen the counterparty before doing anything else.

If the individual does not answer the questions to your satisfaction, if their answers are evasive, or if the information indicates poor screening economics, you should move on.

- Is your biographical information available on LinkedIn or the company website? If not, when can I expect to receive it? Review the biographical information carefully for red flags and complete an internet search.
- Do you have a written option to buy the target company or a signed purchase and sale agreement? When can I anticipate receiving it?
- What was the target company's NIBT for the last two years and the year to date? Was this prepared in accordance with GAAP?
- Does the target company have debt? What is the level of debt, and when is it due? Will the debt be removed at the time of purchase?
- What is the price for acquiring the target company on a debt-free basis, or what are the seller's price expectations if you do not have a written purchase agreement?
- Are you willing to invest your own money in the transaction? What percentage of the purchase price does this represent? What percentage of equity are you expecting in return?
- What will be your role in buying and running the target company?
- Financial investors typically require fifty-one percent equity ownership and/or controlling board interest.

This means you will not have control over the future direction of the target company. Is this acceptable to you?

- What is the target company's existing Vision & Strategy? Is it unique and challenging for competitors to duplicate?
- What is the target company's competitive advantage?
- How can I help you with the transaction besides being a financial investor?

All Companies Can Build M&A Capability

The Size of Your Company is Irrelevant

All major companies have vision, strategy, and M&A capability within their firm, and many consulting companies offer these services for a heavy fee.

Both would like you to believe that a smaller company cannot independently develop this capability. They are mistaken.

You can create a world-class vision, strategy, and M&A capability in your company by using your existing personnel.

You can also use the innovative best practices discussed in this book to get excellent results.

If you intend to do more than one deal or use M&A as a strategy, you should strongly consider building in-house M&A capability. It will help you capture additional value as opposed to using a buy side or sell side business broker for the following reasons:

- They don't know your business. You will spend a lot of valuable time educating them.
- They don't know the potential purchasers. You will have to guide them.
- They don't have access to the necessary information. You will provide it all.
- Without your involvement, they can't write the confidential information memorandum or the management presentation. You will do most of the work.
- They may also provide questionable advice because your incentives are not aligned. You want to complete the right transaction with an attractive price and terms. They want you to complete **any** transaction because they do not get paid unless a transaction closes.

Creating vision, strategy, and M&A capability in your company is a superior alternative. Not only will you be able to complete transactions at a much lower cost, but you will also build in-house capability that will remain after the transaction is complete. You can accomplish this with your existing personnel to a large extent, just as I have done in six different companies.

Chapter 7
Nontraditional Economic Analysis

Sometimes the best acquisitions are the ones you don't make. Just because the price is low doesn't mean you should buy it.

This section of the book is devoted to nontraditional economic analysis, which may appear basic, especially if your current practice is to use complex economic models.

However, these techniques will force you to identify and evaluate those factors that can have the most impact on the economics and success of your transaction.

They will also allow you to quickly eliminate potential acquisition targets that do not measure up to other alternatives and stress test those with the greatest promise.

These principles and techniques are discussed in the following sections:

Qualitative Screening Tools
- Look at the Big Picture
- Competitive Position Matrix Analysis
- Which Option Creates the Most Value
- Attractive Acquisition Characteristics
- Vector In

High-Level Quantitative Metrics

- Evaluate Using Scenarios
- Reconcile Your Model with Reality
- Not All Parts are Equal

Approach with Clear-Eyed Realism

- Beware of Deal Chase

Qualitative Screening Tools

Look at the Big Picture

Many companies rely on elaborate economic models when evaluating a transaction without taking the time to step back and consider the big picture. This is an M&A worst practice.

If a transaction does not look attractive from a big-picture perspective, it does not matter what the models say, no matter how optimistic the results might be.

You can overcome this numbers bias by using **qualitative** screening tools as the first step in your economic analysis.

Competitive Position Matrix Analysis

One of the best qualitative screening tools is the competitive position matrix analysis.

To use this tool, start by identifying those factors that supply a significant competitive edge in the industry you are evaluating. Some examples might be:

- Raw material pricing and supply advantage (stranded supply at lower cost)
- World-scale size (lower cost per unit of production)
- Advanced processing technology (increased yield of higher value products)
- Finished product advantage (superior product characteristics)
- Market advantage (isolated markets permitting higher margins)
- Industry has significant barriers to entry (high capital investment requirements)
- Purchase price is a small fraction of replacement cost (capital advantage)

Now compare the characteristics of your potential acquisition targets against the competitive advantages you have identified. This is easily done in table form, as shown below.

This type of high-level screening analysis will help you quickly decide if a target acquisition has the potential to be attractive without the use of any economic models.

Acquisition Screening:
Competitive Position Matrix Example

Competitive Advantages	Target 1	Target 2
Raw material pricing and supply advantage	Attractive and improving	Attractive
World-scale size	No	Yes
Advanced or new processing technology	Neutral to disadvantaged	Positive
Finished product advantage	Neutral	Positive
Marketing advantage	Disadvantaged	Neutral
Purchase price is a small percentage of replacement cost	No	Yes
Industry has significant barriers to entry	Yes	Yes
Will benefit from macro changes in society (look back at Strategy Reset)	Neutral	Positive
Acquisition prices in this industry are very depressed	Yes	Yes
Synergy with your company	None	Likely
Actionable profit improvement projects	Not apparent	Yes: significant upside
Significant known issues and risks	Material	Neutral

It should be obvious from the example that you would pass on Target 1 and give Target 2 further consideration.

If the acquisition target doesn't have a clear advantage in most of the screening categories you have identified, it is unlikely to supply an acceptable return and is not worth further analysis or consideration.

The only exception might be if there is significant added opportunity that is unique to the target, such as a very depressed acquisition price, synergy with your existing company, or actionable profit improvement projects that are not shared with the other options. However, even then, you should not make a purchase solely on these items because they are not assured and only represent upside potential.

Also, don't ignore known issues or risks. These can easily derail an otherwise attractive acquisition. Consider these as yes/no gating items.

Which Option Creates the Most Value?

Another way to screen potential acquisition candidates is to consider how much value you can create under each option.

Some examples might be:

- Easy to capture value-creation opportunities not pursued by the seller (low-hanging fruit)
- Value creation opportunities that are not available to other purchasers (synergy)
- Structuring options such as a joint venture, merger, or commercial agreement that could create substantial added value
- Offers an opportunity to restructure your existing legal entities consistent with an overall business purpose as part of the transaction (new value chain)

Acquisition Screening: Value Creation Example

Value Creation	Target 1	Target 2
Easy to capture value creation opportunities not pursued by seller	Moderate	Significant
Value creation opportunities that are not available to other purchasers (new IP)	No	Yes
Structuring options such as a joint venture, merger, or commercial agreement that create added value	Neutral	Strong Potential
Opportunity to restructure your existing legal entities consistent with an overall business purpose	No	Yes

Once again, it appears you should pass on Target 1 and focus on Target 2.

Attractive Acquisition Characteristics

A third way to screen potential acquisition candidates is to identify those characteristics that make for an attractive acquisition in your industry, then compare them to your potential target.

Some of the attractive acquisition characteristics that I have used in past analysis include the following:

- High-quality assets
- Strong competitive ranking of the first or second quartile. The third quartile is already under pressure, and the fourth quartile indicates extreme risk and should be avoided
- Significant competitive advantages that are sustainable over time
- Located in an isolated niche market or located in a market with significant barriers to entry
- Current margins are depressed due to cyclical industry overcapacity (which has resulted in a depressed purchase price)
- Attractive position in the business cycle (recession/low industry margins/improving margin point of view)
- Motivated seller either because of a strategic decision or due to Federal Trade Commission (FTC) requirements that are forcing a sale because of a merger or acquisition
- Benefits from macro changes in society, world economy, and industry (look back at the Strategy Reset analysis you completed)
- Brings capability you do not have (assets/brands/IP/markets/products)
- Multiple economic value drivers not tied to one bet
- Financial structuring benefits
- Significant and actionable profit improvement projects

- o Selling, general and administrative expenses (SG&A) reduction
- o Operating cost reduction
- o Raw material cost reduction
- o Finished product margins improved by marketing in different channels
- o Synergy with your existing business

If the acquisition target doesn't match up to your list of attractive acquisition characteristics, it is unlikely to supply an acceptable return and is not worth the commitment of additional time.

Vector In

I recommend you complete all three types of qualitative screening analysis to see if the conclusions are consistent. Assuming they give you the same result, you have a solid green light to move forward. However, if the results are markedly different, stop and figure out why this is happening because it may reveal a material risk you should consider.

The ideal target should have strong competitive advantages, significant new value creation potential, minimal risks, and attractive acquisition characteristics. You can determine this with the qualitative screening tools we have discussed.

High-Level Quantitative Metrics

Evaluate Using Scenarios

Once your qualitative screening tools have identified a potential acquisition target, it is time to perform high-level quantitative analysis.

It is quite easy to use historical earnings as a baseline to generate a large number of economic cases; it is also easy to be fooled by the results.

Your primary focus should be on evaluating the target under a wide range of different macro scenarios to understand their potential effect on standard economic metrics such as net present value (NPV), internal rate of return (IRR), and discounted payout period.

The following are examples of macro events that you should consider building into your scenarios, as well as other factors you identify that are specific to your industry or target:

- Review the Strategy Reset analysis
- Macro changes in society
- Developing trends in the industry
- Competitive threats from outside the industry
- Perspectives from a challenge resource (Cold Eye Review)
- Risks that could significantly damage existing cash flows
- Historically low margins (look for breakeven cash flow after capital expenditure costs)
- Black Swan events
- Ten-year look back using current production with actual historical prices

By running a wide range of different scenarios, you will be able to stress test the potential acquisition for big-picture macro considerations, which can have a substantial impact on your economics. The ten-year lookback also provides a reality check by using actual historical prices.

If the economics are reasonable under all or most of your scenarios, including a historically low margin case and the ten-year look back, the chances are it will be a successful acquisition, perform as expected, and add value to your company.

As far as the specific metrics are concerned, you are looking for an acquisition that displays the following typical characteristics in most of the scenarios:

- A large NPV. A transaction with a small NPV, even if it has a high IRR and a short, discounted payout period, will not materially affect the value of your business.
- High conversion of revenue into EBITDA. This is measured by dividing EBITDA by revenue and is a measure of economic strength.
- High conversion of EBITDA into free cash flow. This is measured by dividing free cash flow by EBITDA and is a measure of strong cash flow generation capability.
- An IRR that is well above your cost of capital.
- A discounted payback period that is less than three years. A shorter payback period reduces the risk of long-term changes in the project materially impacting the economics.

The effort and thoughtfulness you put into developing the macro scenarios will yield the best results, not the precision of the calculations.

Also, use very conservative assumptions when developing each of the scenarios. Most economics end up being overstated due to unexpected downside events.

Reconcile Your Model with Reality

This is one area where calculation precision is paramount.

You must make every effort to ensure the base economic model reflects reality by reconciling the results of the model against the target's net income before tax (NIBT) and free cash flow for both historical years and during each month when new data becomes available during the diligence process. The best practice is to look back as many years as accurate data is available. Five years is very reasonable.

You should also compare the results from any production models you are using against the target's actual production and reconcile any differences.

This ensures both the economic and production models will generate realistic results when you run the different macroeconomic scenarios and will supply a more in-depth understanding of what is actually happening inside the business.

If the models do not match actual production, earnings, and cash flow, then your knowledge of the business is incomplete, and you need to figure out what is actually going on so they can be adjusted to reflect reality. This is a critically important step.

Also, you should create a waterfall table that shows the major changes between the seller's actual financial performance and what you have included in the economics. Now evaluate the table.

- Are your expected improvements realistic?
- Is there an owner for each forecast improvement willing to stake their reputation on capturing the increased earnings?

If the answer to these questions is no, your economics are overly optimistic and should be revised downward.

You must complete this analysis early in the process, or there is a risk you may overpay for the acquisition.

Not All Parts Are Equal

It is also important to understand which of the target's major assets and value chains generate earnings.

It is possible that some parts of the overall business and certain specific assets do not contribute anything to earnings and have negative cash flow. I have seen this situation a number of times.

Also, consider what you learned when completing the financial analysis of value chains during the Strategy Reset. That work made it clear that all parts of a business do not equally contribute earnings.

With this perspective, it may be possible to parse the acquisition into pieces and only buy the strongest parts.

The seller may not like this, but that does not mean they will reject your proposal, especially if you are in a strong negotiating position or they believe the unwanted pieces are valuable and can be sold to someone else or continue to be run.

There is no place for portfolio theory when considering an acquisition. Don't take underperforming assets or value chains unless there is absolutely no alternative and you have factored in the significant expense associated with shutting them down.

They are just a liability that will distract from focusing on the profitable part of the business.

Approach with Clear-Eyed Realism

Beware of Deal Chase

Just because your initial qualitative and quantitative economic analysis shows the acquisition is attractive does not mean your assumptions are achievable.

Approach all acquisitions with clear-eyed realism to avoid deal chase. This occurs when an organization uses overly optimistic economic assumptions or ignores negative factors discovered during due diligence.

This can also occur if the economics are "adjusted" to make them more realistic and easier to sell. This is a mistake that has resulted in many failed acquisitions. Best practice is to require one person to own each bet that is included in the economics, do a Cold Eye Review with an outside resource to challenge your assumptions, and allow the facts to speak for themselves.

Some of the questions you should ask include the following:

- Are the underlying economic bets easily achievable?
- Is there an owner for each economic bet included in the economics?
- Were all the assumptions developed in an unbiased manner?
- Are all the economic assumptions conservative?
- Are the economics inflated to justify the transaction?
- Have all diligence findings been reflected in the purchase price and transaction documents?
- Have you evaluated the full range of scenarios that could affect the business, including an extreme downside case?
- Have you included a ten-year look back using historical prices as a reality check?
- Does the transaction look conservative (e.g., cash flow breakeven even in extreme downside cases)?
- Are the results too good to be true?
- Did you do a Cold Eye Review using an outside resource?

If you feel uncomfortable about any of this, hold off on signing any binding agreements until you have looked everything over with clear-eyed realism.

Chapter 8
Cold Eye Review

The Cold Eye Review is significantly underutilized because it requires humility and a willingness to accept challenges. You must recognize that your team does not know everything and be willing to accept challenges from a person outside your organization.

To conduct a Cold Eye Review, ask a person unfamiliar with your transaction to evaluate what you are considering.

For this to be effective, the individual should understand how to complete the review, come from outside your organization, have full access to the transaction materials, and have enough confidence to speak truth to power.

There is nothing more demoralizing than implementing a new strategy or undertaking a transaction that fails because of factors that could have easily been discovered.

I strongly recommend you use this tool early in the process to review all vision, strategy, and M&A transactions.

A Cold Eye Review is a powerful tool. Your transaction success will improve when you recognize that an outside perspective will bring impartial and valuable insight. It is in your best interests to listen.

The following is an outline of items that should be contemplated in a Cold Eye Review:

Acquisition Challenges You Will Face

- Competitive Position and Strategy Questions
- Macro Diligence Questions
- What You Can Expect from the Purchase and Sale Agreement (PSA)
- What You Can Expect from the Seller
- Review of Seller's Materials and Internal Documents
- Do Not Rely on the Seller's Representations

Acquisition Challenges You Will Face

The biggest challenges companies typically face during an acquisition are:

- Incomplete understanding of the competitive position of the target
- Not considering macro-economic factors
- Missing the few critical diligence items
- Chasing the deal by reducing diligence time and accepting inferior deal terms
  (And the big one...)
- Overpaying

We are going to consider all these challenges in the following sections.

Competitive Position and Strategy Questions

The following are questions concerning competitive position and strategy that the Cold Eye Review should consider:

- Will this acquisition significantly improve your competitive position as a company? If not, why are you doing it?
- Can you run the business with a breakeven cash flow in poor market conditions? If not, the acquisition has elevated risk, and you should negotiate a lower purchase price.
- Are you the logical purchaser for this asset? If not, why are you now in exclusive negotiations? Are you missing a material risk or liability?
- How are you uniquely positioned as a company to improve earnings?
- Have you developed major bets for improving earnings? If not, you are making a high-risk bet on improving market prices and margins, which is totally outside your control.

- Are the sellers marketing other assets? What do they have in common?

    o Are they competitively disadvantaged in some fashion?
    o Are they facing significant downside risks?
    o Do they have production capacity that is not world-scale size?
    o Do they have limited operating flexibility?
    o Is the local business environment difficult?

- What is the competitive position of the asset compared to other facilities?

    o Located in the general region?
    o Which import products into your markets?

    This can be determined in several ways. One measure I have used in the past is EBITDA per unit of raw material input. The higher the EBITDA per unit, the stronger the competitive position of your assets.

- Another way to look at a competitive position is to calculate the cost to manufacture your products and transport them to your primary markets. This is then compared to your competitor's cost to do the same thing. You are at risk if your costs are equal to or higher than your competitor's costs to produce and transport the same products to your primary markets.
- In all cases, you are looking for a first or second-quartile competitive position. A third-quartile position is typical of a company that is under pressure. A fourth-quartile competitive position likely represents a shutdown candidate and should be avoided.

Macro Diligence Questions

The following are examples of macro due diligence questions that the Cold Eye Review should consider:

- What effect would a pandemic have on your product demand and margins?

- o This year?
- o Next year?
- o In the future?

- What effect would climate change have on your production facilities, product demand, and margins?

  - o Rising sea levels?
  - o Severe storm flooding?
  - o Extreme hot temperature events?

- What effect would seismic events have on your assets?

  - o Earthquakes?
  - o Tsunamis?

- What effect would reducing the current raw material (feedstock) supply have on production margins?

  - o Increase feedstock cost?
  - o Reduced yield of high-value products?

- Are product specifications changing? How will this affect your operations and margins?
- Are new government regulations being considered? How will this change your operations and margins?
- Are more stringent environmental regulations being considered for your industry? What effect will this have on your operations and margins?
- Are changes in the predominant form of energy being considered (solar/wind/nuclear)? How will this affect your margins and operations?
- What effect would a change in local, state, or federal government administrations have on your business?
- What effect will an aging population have on demand for your products?
- What are potential new sources of supply for the products that you offer? Consider anything that could change the current supply-demand balance.

  - o Expansions?
  - o Construction of new supply?

- o International imports?
- o Domestic imports?

- Before signing contracts, diligence is required for everything on the purchase agreement schedules. Many of the schedules will have exceptions to the representations, which you need to understand and could result in changes in the purchase price or the agreements. Some examples are:

  - o Assets are in good operating condition except as shown on Schedule X.
  - o There have been no violations of environmental laws during the last two years except as shown on Schedule Y.
  - o There are no liens or debts on the assets except as shown on Schedule Z.

- Before signing contracts, diligence is required for everything on the purchase agreement exhibits. The terms in the exhibits may cause additional costs and ongoing fees, which should result in changes in the purchase price or the agreements. Some examples are:

  - o Inventory measurement and pricing mechanisms
  - o Acceptable levels of inventory and working capital at closing
  - o Ongoing raw material purchase agreement (price and terms)
  - o Intellectual property license
  - o Transition services agreement

What You Can Expect from the Seller's Purchase and Sale Agreement

The following is an explanation of what you can expect from the seller's purchase and sale agreement and its limitations:

- Have you reviewed the purchase and sale agreement (PSA)? Do you understand what it says? It is absolutely necessary that you understand how the PSA works because this is the document that will govern the transaction between signing and closing and after closing. One way to accomplish this is for your M&A lead and M&A attorney to reduce the PSA to a term sheet that would then be reviewed with the entire deal team.

- The seller's representations are useful for finding potential problem areas where you need to focus your due diligence; they are not a substitute for actually doing the work. For example, the agreement may have a general mechanical integrity representation with an associated schedule. The representation itself has limited value, but the schedule may point out things requiring further due diligence.
- You should use the PSA to help flush out information that the seller has not disclosed to you through the confidential information memorandum, management presentation, data room, or Q&A so you can perform the necessary due diligence. Some of the areas to focus on include:
  o Assets being retained by the seller
  o Liabilities being assumed by the purchaser (environmental and other)
  o Contracts that cannot be transferred
  o Contracts that have "take-or-pay" provisions if they are canceled
  o Exceptions to the sufficiency representation
- Closing conditions contained in the purchase and sale agreement should protect you from events that would materially affect your operation. Examples include:
  o Transfer of all government permits needed to run the business
  o All production facilities are operating at full capacity

What You Can Expect from the Seller

The seller is not going to make it easy for you.

It is your responsibility to ask the right questions, complete thorough due diligence, and negotiate the purchase and sale agreement to reflect the appropriate price and language based on what you discover. The seller may:

- Provide minimum disclosure. They will not do your diligence for you. It is up to you to figure out what is missing and what is true and request additional information.
- Not supply year-to-date earnings or monthly earnings as they occur. You should always get this information and reconcile it to your economic models to ensure you are not over-forecasting earnings.
- Use outside experts to supply optimistic earnings and margin projections, especially when their internal viewpoints are quite different. This is one of the reasons why sellers hire outside firms and investment bankers to run their process.
- Answer the exact question you ask and supply nothing more. They may also partially answer your question or ignore it altogether if they don't want to provide the information. It is up to you to request that all information be provided. There should be no exception to this. If they refuse to provide the complete information, you have a major red flag that should prompt further investigation.
- Not comment on the future effects of macroeconomic drivers on the business because the results are "speculative and not a known fact." It is up to you to put together a conservative earnings and margin forecast. Do not use what the seller provides; this is pure fantasy.
- Try to mislead you. It has happened to me on several occasions. You should verify everything. For example, if you are told that the "facilities have operated within their environmental permits for the past two years," verify this by looking at the data. Do not assume you are being supplied with all the information.
- Not provide the schedules and exhibits they want to include as part of the purchase agreement. Without this information, the language in the purchase agreement

can be misleading. For example, the purchase agreement may contain a representation that the seller "has been in compliance with all environmental laws during the past twenty-four months, except as shown on Schedule E." Without reviewing the items on Schedule E, it is not possible to understand their true degree of environmental noncompliance.

- May try to rush your due diligence. This is a major red flag and should cause you to slow things down. The more you know, the more likely you may request a price reduction or change in the contract terms. At the start, they know everything, and you know extraordinarily little. Take your time and complete all the diligence you need to make an informed decision.

Review of Seller's Materials and Internal Documents

In addition to a review of the PSA, you should carefully look over all materials provided by the seller, including the confidential information memorandum (CIM), management presentation, and Q&A responses.

Confidential Information Memorandum

- This is the primary document the seller provides, and it holds a material amount of information about the business. Review everything, but also challenge the information; it is up to you to do the necessary due diligence. It is unlikely the seller will attest to the accuracy or completeness of the document.
- Also, what is missing? What are they not talking about? Some of the typical omissions are:
  o Environmental contamination
  o Safety statistics
  o Outstanding litigation
  o Long-term liabilities

  What is missing may tell you more about the transaction risk than what is actually presented. If the information were positive, it would have been included. All omissions should be carefully evaluated.

Management Presentation

- Is there anything in the management presentation which is materially different from the confidential information memorandum? If so, why?

Q&A

- Are they answering all your questions or skipping certain questions, such as environmental contamination, health and safety reporting, and ongoing litigation?
- Are they partially answering questions in certain areas?
- Insist on the seller completely answering any skipped questions or partial responses.

Your Internal Deal Team Materials

- Look over this material to decide if the deal team is making reasonable economic bets and good macro-economic assumptions.
- Also, look over this material to ensure that significant diligence findings are being directed back to the negotiating team so they can be reflected in the purchase and sale agreement through additional representations, covenants, or a reduction in the purchase price.

Do Not Rely on the Seller's Representations

Under no circumstances should you rely solely on the seller's representations concerning a material fact or condition in place of due diligence.

If the seller's representation turns out to be incomplete or untrue, the amount you can recover may be limited to fifteen to twenty percent of the purchase price, and it may require litigation to enforce your claim, which will distract from running your new business.

Your best course of action is to complete thorough due diligence, including requiring that all your questions be completely answered, so you clearly understand the reality of the situation before signing any documents.

Chapter 9
The Documents Matter

Once the deal euphoria fades, all that remains is your working relationship with the counterparty (which can change) and the transaction documents (which are fixed).

Many M&A and commercial leaders do not have the patience to understand and become involved in drafting the documents.

However, every word and phrase can make a material difference in the ultimate success of the transaction. As a result, **you** should be heavily involved in negotiating and drafting the legal agreements with a focus on ensuring that all material commercial and legal items are appropriately addressed. The following are some examples:

- Commercial matters are incorporated (e.g., the price reflects acceptable economics, a noncompete agreement is included, valuation of inventory and handling of working capital are well thought out, and all the assets necessary to run the business have been included).
- Due diligence findings are reflected in the purchase price, representations, and covenants (e.g., known deficiencies, environmental permits that limit

production, inadequate maintenance, and material contracts that cannot be assigned).

- Division of liability between purchaser and seller is carefully considered and correctly drafted (e.g., environmental liability, residual liability from previous transactions).
- Closing requirements are understood (e.g., hell or high water provisions, FTC requirements, not required to close if major assets are not running at full capacity).
- If pricing formulas or calculations are a part of the agreement, I recommend you include a detailed example that shows the source for all the numbers so there is no chance of confusion.

Also, the deal team should brainstorm a list of everything that can go wrong during the agreement term and include mechanisms for managing each situation in the agreements. Some of the situations you should consider are:

- Business is not generating positive cash flow.
- Facilities are forced to close due to environmental or safety considerations.
- Managing partner is not performing as needed.
- Default on debt.

This will keep disputes to a minimum and help the parties navigate through demanding situations that may arise in the future without creating an adverse relationship.

The following section of the book supplies a detailed look at the most important documents and agreements you will encounter when working on M&A transactions.

Having the discipline to make the documents clear and incorporate all commercial, due diligence, and economic considerations is an M&A best practice that will help minimize post-closing surprises and ensure the transaction performs as expected.

Take the time to review this section in detail. It supplies valuable reference material to help you successfully negotiate and draft your transaction documents.

Acquisition and Divestiture Term Sheet Preparation

- Conduct Due Diligence on Your Counterparty
- Main Term Sheet Components

  - Disclaimer
  - Structure
  - Price Paid
  - Inventory/Working Capital
  - Assets Acquired
  - Assets Excluded
  - Shared Assets
  - Debt and Liens
  - Division of Liability
  - Representations
  - Indemnity
  - Due Diligence
  - Human Resources Matters
  - Conduct of Business (Covenant)
  - Regulatory Approvals
  - Parent Guarantee
  - Closing Conditions
  - Termination
  - Other Agreements
  - Board Approval
  - Stockholder Support Agreement
  - Assignment
  - Legal matters

Joint Venture Term Sheet Preparation

(Acquiring a new business by forming a joint venture)

- Main Term Sheet Components
  All the material outlined above, plus the following:

  - Vision/Principles/Purpose
  - Duration of the Venture

- o Capitalization of the Venture
- o Capital Contributions
- o Cash Distributions
- o Members' Rights
- o Appointment to the Board of Managers
- o Board of Managers' Authority
- o Officers' Authority
- o Sales to Third Parties
- o Purchases and Sales between Members of the Venture
- o Other Transactions between Members
- o Tax Matters

- Drafting the Joint Venture Agreements

Evaluate Seller's CIM, Data Room, and Presentations

- Gauge the Integrity of the Seller through Their Sales Materials

Confidential Information Memorandum Preparation

(Used when divesting a business, attracting a joint venture partner, bringing together a merger, or inviting venture capital/private equity investment)

- Teaser
- Elements of the Confidential Information Memorandum

  - o Disclaimer
  - o Executive Summary
  - o Technology/IP Considerations
  - o Competitive Position and Risk
  - o Financial Information and Economics
  - o Other Potential Sources of Value
  - o Structure and Governance
  - o Contact Information
  - o Appendix

Acquisition and Divestiture Term Sheet Preparation

When used properly, a term sheet will allow you to quickly decide if an agreement can be reached on the major commercial components of a transaction.

If it is not possible to reach agreement in a four-to-five-page term sheet, there is no chance of negotiating the main transaction documents, which can be hundreds of pages long.

It is in your best interests to discover this early in the process before committing considerable time and resources to the project.

Both companies' M&A and commercial leaders should be the primary negotiators when developing the term sheet. This is because the focus should be on the commercial components of the transaction rather than legal matters.

As a second step, it is essential that attorneys and the board of directors also supply input and sign off on the final document.

When completed, the term sheet will become a roadmap for putting together the overall transaction agreements and will help prevent attempts to re-trade the deal terms previously agreed upon.

Developing a term sheet also ensures that everyone in your company is on the same page concerning the essential components of the transaction. The document will help you quickly and easily explain the major deal terms to get their input before negotiations begin and provide updates after discussions are underway.

However, there is also an inflection point of diminishing returns when putting together a term sheet. Reach an agreement on all the major commercial terms and division of liability questions. When that is accomplished, it is time to draft the definitive agreements.

Having the discipline to negotiate a term sheet before drafting the transaction agreements is an M&A best practice.

Conduct Due Diligence on Your Counterparty

Before beginning discussions with any counterparty, you should carefully perform due diligence on the company and the officers.

Some of your diligence questions should include:

- Is the company financially sound?
- Does it have a good reputation in the industry?
- Have you run a check on the company and the officers through government databases?
- Are there any legal red flags? (e.g., Foreign Corrupt Practices Act violations)
- Does it have significant ongoing litigation?
- Are there negative internet articles about its business practices?
- Does it understand the liabilities associated with its business (such as environmental contamination)?
- Are they answering your questions fully and truthfully?

There is no upside to getting involved with a questionable counterparty. Do yourself a favor and only do business with companies and individuals that have a solid reputation and act with integrity.

Main Term Sheet Components

At a minimum, it is recommended the term sheet includes the following items, which are a part of all M&A transactions.

You should also include other commercial and legal matters specific to your situation, so the roadmap for drafting the transaction documents will be complete.

Disclaimer

The term sheet should always include a disclaimer saying the document is a "nonbinding indication of interest, not an offer to purchase or sell." Only the final signed agreements should be legally binding.

Vision/Principles/Purpose

It is useful to start the term sheet with a vision statement. This will guide how all the other matters are managed. When putting together the vision, principles, and purpose statement, it may be helpful to ask the following questions:

- How will the seller be paid (cash/stock/contingency payment based on performance)?
- How will liabilities be divided (assumed by purchaser or kept by seller)?
- How will assets be divided (transferred to purchaser or kept by seller)?
- How will the business be managed between signing and closing?

Structure

Define the type of transaction at the beginning of the term sheet because this will affect all the following provisions. Will this be an asset purchase, stock purchase, merger, joint venture, or something else?

Price Paid

What price is being paid to the seller?

- Price for real property, plant, and equipment
- Price for shares
- Contingency payment based on post-closing performance
- As a seller, you should not accept a financing contingency. The purchaser should have their financing in place before

signing the agreements or be prepared to deposit a significant portion of the purchase price in escrow, which would be forfeited if they failed to close

Inventory/Working Capital

Payment for inventory and working capital is a major item in most transactions. Consider the following:

- Will there be a separate payment for the inventory of raw materials and finished products?
- Generally, both accounts receivable and accounts payable should be kept by the seller unless you are buying equity. This simplifies a number of items in the transaction.
- Inventory should be valued at the lower of the seller's production cost, acquisition price, or market price. A separate schedule is usually needed to define the pricing mechanism due to the complexity involved. As a purchaser, you should resist purchasing inventory at full market price without a discount because the company will not make a profit when selling this inventory to customers. If you cannot reach an agreement on this concept, ask the seller to completely liquidate all inventory before closing. That way, all production and sales after closing will contribute to earnings.
- Obsolete, off-specification, or unmarketable inventory should not be purchased. It actually has a negative value.
- Will there be a price adjustment +/- for working capital/inventory outside of a specific target range? You should not agree to pay for an unlimited level of working capital or inventory because excess working capital and inventory must be reduced before the business can run at full capacity.

Assets Acquired

What assets, equity, or value will be acquired by the purchaser? All the following should be considered:

- Equity
- All the assets described in the confidential information memorandum and management presentation
- Everything that is necessary to conduct business in the normal course as it has been operated in the last twenty-four months. This is important in any transaction but especially salient when assets or businesses are carved out of a larger entity (sufficiency representation)
- Plants, process units, equipment, buildings, tanks, caverns, docks, pipelines, truck, and rail loading facilities, tangible personal property
- Catalysts, chemicals, packaging, and spare parts
- Real property, buffer property, owned or leased
- Offices, buildings
- Right-of-way agreements, easements, permits
- Contracts and agreements (written or otherwise)
- Government licenses and permits
- IP, patents, formulas, trademarks, domain names, know-how
- Rolling stock, vehicles, rail cars
- Computers and software
- Data, records, plans, manuals, drawings, and specifications
- Customer lists and marketing studies
- Strategic studies
- Lease of land or equipment from the seller
- Exclusive development rights in a specific region
- Other assets specific to this transaction

The lease of land and plant from the seller should be reflected in a lower purchase price since the purchaser must make future payments and does not have outright title.

You should also review the CIM, management presentation, and the entire data room, including updates and written Q&A, to find other items that should be specified.

Assets Excluded

What assets, equity, or value are being kept by the seller?

- Real property, plant, and equipment?
- Equity (e.g., preferred stock)?
- IP and know-how?
- Other assets specific to this transaction?

Excluded assets should be reflected in a lower purchase price unless it is something you do not want to buy because of underlying liabilities or potential future costs (e.g., facilities that are uncompetitive and may need to be shut down).

Shared Assets

What assets will be shared by the parties after closing?

- Real property, plant, and equipment?
- IP and know-how?
- Development rights in a specific region?

Shared assets should be avoided if possible because each will require a separate operating agreement and can result in future conflicts over the allocation of use between the parties, responsibility for capital expenditures, operating practices, the appointment of personnel, and other matters.

Alternatively, it may be better to have one party or the other retain the shared asset and put in place a long-term agreement to provide services to the other party.

Debt and Liens

Define if the seller will repay all company debt and remove all liens from the assets before closing.

If debt and liens are not removed, the purchase price should be reduced accordingly.

Division of Liability

Allocation of liabilities between the parties will be heavily negotiated and should be clearly defined in the term sheet.

Most liabilities will transfer to the purchaser if stock is being bought. There may be a partial transfer of liability to the purchaser if assets are being purchased.

Define who will be responsible for liabilities resulting from the seller's pre-closing activities. The purchaser will want the seller to remain responsible for all liabilities resulting from pre-closing activities, including environmental liabilities. The seller will prefer to transfer all liabilities to the purchaser. Consider the following:

- Environmental contamination (known and unknown)
- Natural resource damage claims
- Superfund claims
- Pre-closing violations of environmental, health and safety laws, and any violations discovered within twelve months after closing
- Pre-closing violations of antitrust laws that are discovered within six months after closing
- Off-site disposal of hazardous and non-hazardous waste
- Products manufactured before closing
- Products sold before closing
- Contracts and permits which are not transferred
- Taxes
- Accounts payable
- Debt and liens
- Employee benefit plans and employee matters
- Claims arising out of the pre-closing condition of assets
- Prior acquisitions and dispositions
- Seller obligations to shareholders, partners, investors
- Other liabilities specific to this transaction

Review the CIM, management presentation, and entire data room, including updates and written Q&A, to find other items that should be specified.

In some cases, the purchaser may accept responsibility for certain known environmental liabilities from the seller (if the level of environmental contamination is low), subject to an indemnity provided by the seller for unknown environmental contamination. In this situation, the seller may require certain use restrictions to help limit their future costs (land deed restricted for industrial use, no use of groundwater, and environmental testing limited to that required by law). If the purchaser does not follow the use restrictions, that part of the seller's indemnity will be void.

In the situation where cash flow generated by the target is low, there is significant environmental contamination, or there is the potential for a large amount of unknown environmental contamination, the purchaser should consider requiring the seller to remain responsible for all environmental liabilities resulting from pre-closing activities subject to the use restrictions discussed above.

Any liabilities that are transferred to the purchaser, including those covered by an indemnity, should be reflected in a lower purchase price versus a transaction free of liabilities resulting from pre-closing activities.

Representations

These are statements made by the seller or purchaser concerning certain facts that are material to the transaction. Consider including the following:

- **Sufficiency:** The purchaser will receive everything necessary to conduct business in the normal course as it has been operating for the last twenty-four months. This is important in any transaction but especially salient when assets or businesses are carved out of a larger entity. This representation will force disclosure of things being retained by the seller that will have to be replaced by the purchaser so they can be bridged with a long-term service agreement or replaced. This may also reduce the purchase price depending on the cost to bridge or replace the missing items.

- **Condition of Assets:** The assets are in good operating condition and have been maintained following standard industry practice.
- **Financial Statements:** The financial statements provided by the company are materially correct and were prepared in accordance with GAAP.
- **Compliance with Laws:** The assets and business were run in compliance with all laws, rules, and regulations, including environmental laws.
- **Production Capacity:** Production rates and plant capacities shown in the management presentation can be achieved and sustained when operations are running normally.
- **Organization/Good Standing/No Conflicts/Title to Assets:** The seller has the necessary power to complete the transaction.

Beware if there is pushback on any of these items; they are all critical for the successful performance of the business. Any exceptions to the representations should be listed in a Disclosure Schedule, which allows you to conduct meaningful diligence (e.g., except as shown on Schedule 1, the assets are in good operating condition).

It is very important that you understand the impact of all exceptions to these representations. Depending on the severity of the items, a reduction in the purchase price may be needed, or you may choose to walk away from the transaction altogether.

Also, be careful accepting assets that are sold "as is where is" with no representations or warranty. In this case, you must perform comprehensive due diligence concerning the condition of the assets, their ability to perform as expected, and any liabilities you may be taking on.

Indemnity

Indemnity is an obligation to compensate the purchaser or seller for a specific loss.

Typical indemnities cover breaches of representations and warranties, breaches of covenants, and agreements to pay for costs resulting from certain pre-closing activities (e.g., environmental contamination).

Each indemnity may have a different deductible, time limit, and dollar cap. For example, it is common to have an environmental indemnity separate from the general indemnity, which has different terms and a separate cap.

The indemnity for breaches of the representations is typically capped at ten to fifteen percent of the purchase price. The indemnity for breaches of the fundamental representations is typically capped at the full purchase price.

Indemnification for seller-retained liabilities and breaches of covenants should be uncapped and without a time limit.

Due Diligence

An agreement must be reached concerning the level of due diligence that will be allowed. Some of the things you should consider are:

- Time period (sixty days)
- Access to data / information (immediate and complete)
- Access to facilities (immediate and complete)
- Access to knowledgeable company personnel (well before signing and not restricted to the other party's advisors or senior officers who may have limited actual knowledge)
- Acceptability of invasive environmental diligence such as a Phase II environmental investigation (sampling of soil and groundwater)

All diligence should be completed <u>before</u> the purchase agreements are signed. Do not accept a post-signing due diligence walk-away provision. If you are the seller, this is just a free option for the purchaser to walk away from the deal without penalty any time before closing. It is far better to let the purchaser complete their due diligence before signing.

Be careful of a situation where the seller wants to severely limit your due diligence access or force an accelerated due diligence schedule (except in a public company situation). This may be a sign of material problems they do not want you to discover.

Human Resources Matters

Employee considerations are important in every transaction.

The seller will want to understand if you will hire all the employees and who will be responsible for severance costs for anyone you do not take.

The purchaser will want to interview and select only those employees who meet their requirements. All the remaining employees would be terminated as a part of the closing process and remain the seller's responsibility.

There should also be provisions that prevent the seller from transferring or hiring away the management and technical employees you will need to run the business.

If there is a union, consideration must be given to adopting the labor agreement.

Conduct of Business (Covenant)

These are the seller's promises to conduct the business in a certain fashion between signing the agreements and closing the transaction.

You should consider requiring the seller to:

- Operate the business in the ordinary course

- Maintain the assets in the ordinary course, including making planned capital and maintenance expenditures
- Comply with applicable laws
- Not sell or dispose of any material assets
- Not add debt or liens
- Not change or cancel any material contract or permit
- Not issue more equity

Regulatory Approvals

Depending on the size of the transaction, antitrust approval may be needed.

In this circumstance, the seller may want the purchaser to take on all risks associated with meeting the government's requirements, including selling existing assets or businesses or litigating challenges. This is sometimes called a "Hell or High Water" provision and should be rejected because it could force you to dismantle part of your current business to complete this transaction.

Parent Guarantee

If the purchaser or seller is a newly formed company, has a low credit rating, or will become a shell entity after the transaction, you should require a guarantee from the parent company to ensure the purchaser meets its obligations under the agreements (e.g., indemnity, break fee).

If this is not possible, it may be acceptable to hold back a sizable part of the purchase price in an escrow agreement. This is not an option in the case of extensive environmental contamination, which can take many years to define and remediate.

Closing Conditions

Closing conditions should be limited to those items that are needed to ensure the integrity of the transaction. Unnecessary closing conditions increase the chance the transaction will fail.

Some reasonable closing conditions might be:

- Customary government and regulatory approvals have been received (e.g., Hart-Scott-Rodino Act)
- Permits necessary to run the facilities have been transferred or acquired
- Consents for certain material contracts have been received
- Debt has been repaid, and liens removed
- Casualty loss above a certain amount has been cured
- Accuracy of reps and warranties
- Compliance with covenants and other agreements in the transaction documents
- No Material Adverse Effect (MAE) has occurred or is likely to occur
- All facilities are running at normal rates
- Other closing conditions specific to this transaction

Unreasonable closing conditions might be:

- *Ability to secure financing.* This adds another layer of approval from a financial institution. The purchaser should arrange financing in advance. I suggest you specifically state there will not be a financing contingency.
- *Due diligence 'out.'* This is a free option for the purchaser to exit the transaction without penalty at any time before closing. I suggest you state that all diligence will be completed before the Asset Purchase Agreement (APA) is signed, and there will not be a due diligence exit option.
- *Approval by the board of managers or board of directors.* This should be completed before signing the definitive agreements rather than as a closing condition. If the

board is not supportive, you want to discover this before committing considerable time and resources.

Termination

Provisions for terminating the agreement need to be defined, so it is possible to walk away from the transaction under certain circumstances.

Common termination provisions include:

- If signing has not occurred by a specific date (term sheet only)
- If closing has not occurred by a specific date (Outside Date in final agreements)
- Declaration of bankruptcy by either party

In addition, you might want to consider a liquidated damage break fee (a specific dollar amount) that would be paid if either party does not complete the transaction when all closing conditions have been met.

Other Agreements

You should also consider the need for other agreements that may be required to ensure the business can continue to operate in the normal way.

Some of these might be:

- Transition Services
- Feedstock Supply
- IP License (exclusive, perpetual, and without royalty or use fee)
- Toll Manufacturing in another facility
- Product Purchase
- Noncompete Agreement

Board Approval

A board review should be required when the term sheet is agreed upon (to ensure they are informed).

Board approval should be secured before signing the definitive agreements.

For a stock transaction, unanimous board approval and delivery of a certain level of shareholder consent may be required under the company's Shareholder Agreement.

Stockholder Support Agreement

This is an agreement between the purchaser and target company shareholders where the shareholders agree to the following:

- Approve the transaction
- Amend or waive provisions in the Shareholder Agreement as necessary to facilitate the proposed transaction
- Agree to pay in proportion to their shareholdings any shortfall in the working capital

Assignment

Assignments should be carefully negotiated.

As a purchaser, you want the ability to assign the transaction documents in whole or in part to a future purchaser of the business or assets without the seller's consent.

This is needed to ensure you can transfer the seller's indemnities and the seller's parent guarantee to a future purchaser so you are not in the middle of future claims between the original seller and the new purchaser.

Legal Matters

This section is added as a second step only after the major commercial terms are agreed upon. If it is not possible to reach an agreement on the major commercial terms discussed above, the legal matters will not change the situation.

Joint Venture Term Sheet Preparation

Acquiring a New Business by Forming a Joint Venture

This section is included because forming a joint venture is another way to acquire a new business. It is also one of the most challenging structures to put in place.

In addition to the acquisition term sheet components discussed above, the following items should be considered when constructing a joint venture term sheet.

Main Term Sheet Components

Vision/Principles/Purpose

It is useful to start the term sheet with a vision statement. This will help guide how other matters are managed. Some of the questions you should answer are:

- What is the overall Vision & Strategy for the venture (look back at the Strategy Reset discussion)?
- How will profit be created?
- How will the parties work together?
- Who will be the managing partner?
- How will equity be divided?
- How will cash dividends be divided?
- How will board rights be divided?
- Will the members deal with each other in good faith?

Duration of the Venture

The duration of the venture (number of years) and whether the venture can be liquidated are particularly important considerations that will affect all other aspects of the transaction.

If possible, set up the venture with a perpetual term and limited liquidation provisions (e.g., bankruptcy).

This will be most attractive to future purchasers and avoids disputes at the end of the first term concerning how to wind up the venture or if it should be extended.

You can always sell your member units to the other owners or a third party if you no longer wish to be involved.

Capitalization of the Venture

You will need to decide how the venture will initially be capitalized. This will be a major point of negotiation between the parties. Some of the options are:

- Cash contributions
- Asset contributions (e.g., IP, patents, know-how)
- Equity contributions
- Debt issued

Also, under what circumstances can new debt be placed on the venture?

- After the first commercial plant is constructed and running at full capacity?
- Only within certain financial coverage ratios?

These items should be thought through and included in the term sheet.

Capital Contributions

The venture may need capital contributions until internal cash flow is sufficient to sustain operations.

Deciding which members will make the first and ongoing capital contributions should be carefully considered because certain arrangements can dilute your equity in the venture.

Some of the considerations are:

- Which members will contribute the first capital to fund NewCo's operation and plant construction through the R&D, demonstration pilot plant, and first commercial plants? Financial members only or all members?

- Is there any limit to this initial level of capital contribution in dollars or years?
- What happens if more capital is needed beyond what was anticipated (e.g., the financial members will make the additional capital contribution or exit the venture through one of the agreed upon mechanisms—put at nominal value, sale to a third party)?
- Is there any limit to the level of capital contribution associated with starting up more plants in dollars or years?
- Can the venture issue debt to fund capital requirements?
- Will the relative ownership percentage of the members change depending on the level of capital contributed (e.g., if an owner decides not to contribute additional capital, their ownership percentage will be proportionally diluted)?

Cash Distributions

When the venture achieves positive cash flow, decisions must be made concerning how to use surplus funds. Specifically, when will cash distributions be made to the members, and how will the distributions be allocated? Some of the items to consider are:

- Will distributions be made based on ownership percentage?
- Will ongoing cash requirements of the business limit distributions?
- Will cash distributions be limited to surplus cash generated from operations, or can surplus cash received from issuing debt be distributed to the members?
- Will distributions require that certain debt coverage ratios be maintained?

Members' Rights

The members, the board of managers, and the officers of the company will oversee management of the venture.

The venture members may want to reserve certain actions for the unanimous approval of all members. Consider if the following actions require unanimous approval of all members or if the board can manage them.

-   Sale of the venture
-   Initial public offering (IPO) of the venture
-   Approval of any guarantees from the owners of the company
-   Sale of assets in excess of $5 million
-   Settlement or initiation of any litigation above $5 million
-   Bankruptcy or liquidation of the venture
-   Contracts between the members
-   Compensation of board members
-   Change in the size (+/-) of the board of managers
-   Change in the capital structure such as issue or redemption of member units and issue or redemption of debt
-   Allow liens on any of the assets
-   Admit a new member
-   Make capital contributions beyond what was previously agreed
-   Issue debt
-   Changes in cash dividend policy
-   Establishment of cash reserves
-   Lend funds to employees or directors
-   Rebuild if a casualty loss exceeds a certain level
-   Change the form of the company
-   Growth or changes in the company through acquisitions, joint ventures, mergers, stock swaps, or investments in other companies
-   Entering a new type of business
-   Modify accounting policies and choice of auditor
-   Amend the venture agreements

There are other actions that each member should be able to take on a unilateral basis. Consider the following:

- Appoint individuals to the board of managers for the seats that they control.
- Sale of member units to a third party.
- Execute right of first offer (ROFO) or right of first refusal (ROFR).
- Purchases and sales between members (put/call/put-nominal value/buy-sell/drag-along/tag-along).

Appointment to the Board of Managers

The board of managers is the next layer of management. Consider how the board will be appointed and function.

- How many board seats will each member control?
- How will board members be appointed?
- Will the board members have a liability policy paid by the venture?

Board of Managers' Authority

Except for actions reserved for the members, the board of managers should have the authority to manage the business. This could include:

- Make cash calls to the members per the venture agreements.
- Pay a cash distribution to the members per the venture agreements.
- Approve contracts in excess of $2 million per year or for more than two years in duration.
- Issue letters of credit.
- Approve plans to invest in the plant's infrastructure.
- Approve plans to build more plants.
- Approve major capital expenditures.
- Approve annual operating budget.
- Approve annual capital budget.
- Approve capital expenditures above $2 million.
- Approve company operating practices (e.g., regulatory compliance).

- Approve company staffing and organizational structure.
- Addition or changes in management and officers.
- Approve employee and officer compensation levels.
- Approve collective bargaining agreements.
- Approve major changes in policies and procedures for running the business.
- Approve entering into major agreements (above certain dollar and time limits).
- Review the performance of the company.
- Approve financial statements and tax filings.

Officers' Authority

The company's officers should have the authority to run the company on a day-to-day basis. At a minimum, this should include the following:

- Responsibility for profit and loss
- Manage agreements with third parties and between members (if any)
- Prepare materials needed for approval by the board of managers (see above)
- Respond to requests from the board of managers
- Ensure the venture is run in compliance with all laws, rules, and regulations
- Ensure the venture is operated safely
- Ensure the venture is run in compliance with environmental regulations
- Enter into agreements (below specific dollar and time limits)
- Recommend staffing and salary levels for approval by the board of managers

Sales to Third Parties

Provisions for sales to third parties can include the following options as well as others:

- **Sale of the Venture**: This provision allows either party to cause the entire venture to be sold. This option should not be available until well into the life of the project and only after the owners have received cash distributions that result in an acceptable return on their original investment.

- **IPO of the Venture**: This provision allows either party to cause the entire venture to be offered for sale under an initial public stock offering. This option should also not be available until well into the project's life and only after the owners have received cash distributions that result in an acceptable return on their original investment. It should also include provisions that limit its use to specific circumstances where an IPO is likely to result in a higher value than a sale to a third party.

- **Right of First Offer:** This provision is used at the start of the sale process and requires the selling member to first offer their units to the other venture owners before they can be offered for sale to a third party. If the other members decline the purchase at the offered price, the selling member is free to sell their units to a third party at the offered price within an agreed-upon price band (plus/minus).

- **Right of First Refusal:** This provision is used at the end of the sale process and requires the selling member to first negotiate the sale price and terms with a third party before offering the same sales price and terms to the other members of the venture. This provision should be avoided if possible because it tends to depress the sale price. The third-party purchaser must complete the work necessary to finish the purchase, including due diligence and negotiating the agreements, and could still lose the sale to the other members of the venture.

Purchases and Sales between Members of the Venture

Handling of purchases and sales between members is also complex and can include, among others, the following options:

- **Call – Formula Price**: This provision allows either member to buy (call) the other member's interest at a price that is set using a predetermined formula.

    Items to consider when negotiating this provision include:

    - The pricing formula should be straightforward, not complex, and market-based. Avoid forward-looking NPV calculations because they require multiple assumptions and are inherently inaccurate.
    - Decide the first date when the call can be executed. This should be sufficiently far in advance that the economic potential and corresponding market value have been fully realized. Consider five to ten years.

- **Put – Formula Price:** This provision allows either member to sell (put) their interest to the other member at a price that is set using a predetermined formula.

    The items to consider when negotiating this provision are the same as for the call:

    - The pricing formula should be straightforward, not complex, and market-based. Avoid forward-looking NPV calculations because they require multiple assumptions and are inherently inaccurate.
    - Decide the first date when the put can be executed. This should be sufficiently far in advance that the economic potential and corresponding market value have been fully realized. Consider five to ten years.

- **Put – Nominal Value:** This provision allows either member to sell (put) their interest to the other member at a significantly reduced price agreed upon in advance.

  Items to consider when negotiating this provision include:

  - The only time a member will use this provision is when they believe the future of the venture is in question and they want to get out quickly. Carefully consider if you want to allow this.
  - Also, the price should be high enough to discourage an unhelpful exit and supply some cushion for the remaining venture members. The price of one dollar is unacceptable, and the full market value is too high.

- **Buy or Sell:** This provision allows the member that starts the buy-sell process to either buy the other member's interest at the offer price or sell their interest at the same price.

  Items to consider when negotiating this provision include:

  - Decide if you want to offer this choice if one party realistically cannot buy the other party's interest. In this case, the larger member could force the smaller member to accept a below-market purchase price.
  - Decide the first date when the provision can be executed. This should be sufficiently far in advance so the economic potential and corresponding market value have been fully realized. Otherwise, there is no way to gauge if the offer is reasonable. Consider five to ten years.

- **Drag-Along:** This provision allows the member selling their interest to a third party to include (drag-along) the other members' units in the sale under identical terms.

  Items to consider when negotiating this provision include:

- Is it acceptable for you to be forced to sell your units? This also works in reverse.
- Keep in mind this would effectively remove any right of first refusal you might have but should not affect your right of a first offer if the language is carefully drafted.
- Decide the first date when the drag-along can be executed. This should be sufficiently far in advance so that the economic potential and corresponding market value have been fully realized. Consider five to ten years.
- This concept allows the entire venture to be sold at one time, increasing the attractiveness to a purchaser.

- **Tag-Along**: This provision allows the member who is not selling their interest to a third party to include their units in the sale (tag-along) if they find the terms attractive.

  Items to consider when negotiating this provision include:

  - Is it acceptable for the other party to include their units as part of a sale? This also works in reverse.
  - Decide the first date when the tag-along can be executed. This should be done far enough in advance so that the economic potential and corresponding market value have been fully realized. Consider five to ten years.

The sales agreement that will be used for purchases and sales between members (Put/Call/Buy or Sell) should be developed and included as an attachment to the venture's legal agreements. This will prevent disagreements concerning the form and terms of the transfer if it is needed at a future date.

Other Transactions between Members

Sometimes transactions between members are needed because the venture is located on or adjacent to facilities owned or operated by one of the members (e.g., chemical plant) or because they rely on one of the members for feedstock or services needed to run the business.

These transactions can be complex, requiring a separate stand-alone agreement, so they will only be briefly mentioned.

-   Operating services provided by one party to another (e.g., maintenance, wastewater treating, steam, dock use)
-   Business services provided by one party to another (e.g., management, marketing, environmental health, safety)
-   Raw material provided by one party to another (e.g., specialized feedstocks)
-   Products bought by one party from another (e.g., byproducts, finished products)

Tax Matters

Tax planning is one area that should be given careful consideration because of the complexity associated with tax laws.

Outside experts can manage this, but it may be advisable to appoint one member as the "tax matters partner" if they have the necessary expertise. The tax matters partner would:

-   Prepare and file tax returns for the venture.
-   Provide tax planning associated with major changes in the venture, such as expansion plans and sales of the venture.

This service may be provided to the venture without cost or through a separate service agreement.

Other Matters

This is not an all-inclusive list of items for the term sheet; it is an outline of matters that are discussed before forming a venture.

Each transaction is different, so you must think through all the factors associated with your particular circumstance and include those that are most important.

Examples of other items you may want to consider include:

- Will there be an operating partner?
- How will a casualty loss be managed?
- When does dissolution/liquidation occur?
- Under what conditions does Force Majeure apply?

Drafting the Joint Venture Agreements

Drafting the final joint venture agreements will be a significant undertaking. It is common for such agreements to be hundreds or even thousands of pages in length.

Hopefully, you have followed the M&A Best Practices for negotiating a term sheet that can now be used as a guide for developing definitive agreements. This will simplify the drafting and make the process much less confrontational.

The definitive agreements can be organized using the term sheet categories or grouped in other ways. The most important thing is to ensure that all the items are covered.

Evaluate Seller's CIM, Data Room, and Presentations

Gauge the Integrity of the Seller through Their Sales Materials

In addition to considering the facts concerning an acquisition, you should evaluate the integrity of the seller through their sales process.

Carefully listen to what they say and disclose, as well as what they don't say and withhold.

Are they approaching the sale in a transparent and forthright manner with full and complete disclosure? Some specific things to watch are discussed below.

Are there holes in the confidential information memorandum and data room, such as the seller not providing the following:

- Financial statements (not pro forma statements or projections)
- Litigation disclosure
- Lost time accidents statistics
- Environmental notice of violation statistics
- Characterization of known environmental contamination
- Disclosure concerning underground storage tanks
- Additional information in the data room after it is requested
- Disclosure concerning the need for significant capital expenditures in future years

Are answers to Q&A questions incomplete or carefully parsed to present only a part of the information or tilt the answer in the most favorable light?

Does the management presentation feel like a carefully choreographed "show" with little substance?

Do they avoid directly answering tough questions or do their answers change if they are challenged?

If any of these red flags are present, I strongly recommend you consider backing away from the transaction.

It is difficult enough to find and complete an attractive acquisition without dealing with a seller who lacks integrity.

Confidential Information Memorandum Preparation

Constructing a confidential information memorandum (CIM) is an important tool for divesting a business, attracting a joint venture partner, bringing together a merger, or inviting venture capital/private equity investment.

This outline for constructing a CIM includes nontraditional features that are especially important to venture capital and private equity firms and should be considered in all applications.

The CIM allows you to lay out a vision for the business and promote attractive features.

It is also important that you address the major risk factors associated with the business. This may seem counterintuitive, and the traditional format sometimes glosses over risks or does not cover them. However, this is a missed opportunity because the risks will eventually become known as the counterparty performs its due diligence.

By addressing concerns up front, you have an opportunity to present your perspective and defuse the issues, so they do not become a major obstacle in completing the transaction. In addition, if these items are a significant problem for the counterparty, it is best to discover this before devoting a lot of time and resources to a transaction that will not move forward.

Being straightforward in this fashion builds credibility with the counterparty and will strengthen your negotiating position when drafting the agreements.

Teaser

To run a robust M&A process and find the best counterparties, you will need a teaser that can be distributed to potential parties before the CIM.

The teaser is a nonconfidential abbreviated form of the CIM and is developed after it is completed.

If a company expresses interest after reviewing the teaser, you will ask them to sign a nondisclosure agreement before sending the CIM and starting the full M&A process.

Elements of the Confidential Information Memorandum

The document should contain the following elements in the order presented below.

The company should prepare the items in this outline with input from all groups that engage in running the business.

Disclaimer (prepared by your attorney)

The disclaimer is boilerplate legal language that will be at the front of the document and should include the following concepts:

- CIM is confidential.
- Material contained in the CIM that was provided by third-party sources is identified when used.
- You may not rely on the CIM when evaluating the transaction; you must perform your own due diligence.
- The CIM may not have all the information that is relevant to you.
- The document has forward-looking projections based on the subjective perspective of the company. Actual results are likely to be different for the simple reason that it is impossible to predict the future.
- All liability should be expressly disclaimed.

Executive Summary

The CIM should begin with an executive summary that provides a high-level description of the business and the opportunity. This should be one page at the most. All the items contained in the summary will be discussed in greater detail later in the document.

- General description of the business

  o How does/will the business make money?
  o Discussion of current and potential markets.

- Financial summary

  o It is imperative that you state your economics in summary form at the beginning of the document without a lot of technical details.
  o Remember your audience. They are primarily financial people and will be focused on understanding if the project has the potential to create significant economic value with a moderate level of risk.

- Technology/IP considerations/Plant overview (current or future).

  o This should be done at a high level without a lot of details.

- Transaction flowchart

  o This is an arrow diagram explaining the proposed transaction: what each group is contributing (e.g., IP/cash/marketing) and what they get back in the form of equity, rights, or payment.
  o Strive for simplicity and realism in a balanced transaction (not one-sided).

- Startup flowchart

  o For a startup, include an outline of the steps from now through full-scale production and the funding requirements for each step.

      ○ This is needed so the cash partner understands the total investment they are making.

- Diagram of the final company structure

      ○ Simplicity is best.
      ○ Recommend you propose a structure that can be achieved in one transaction rather than two or three steps. Complexity is a killer in deal structuring.

Technology/IP Considerations

This section explains how your technology compares to the competition and if it is defensible. You should include the following:

- A general explanation of the technology. Put the technical details in the appendix or skip them altogether. They will hire an expert later in the process to examine the technology.
- How does this project compare to alternatives that accomplish the same goals using different technology? Does it have a significant advantage from lower capital investment, lower operating costs, higher yields, better quality products, or lower sales price to the end consumer? Prepare a side-by-side comparison in table form.
- Are there competitors in the same space who use similar technology? You must understand this situation and be prepared to discuss why this is not a concern.
- An explanation of how intellectual property is protected or will be protected (e.g., patents have been awarded to the individuals involved or know-how is invested in the individuals that will become part of the management team).

All this should be at an elevated level but with enough substance, so it is clear you know what you are talking about. The technical details can be covered in later discussions.

Competitive Position and Risk

The counterparty will want to understand how this business/technology compares to the competition and if it is defensible. You should include the following:

- Competitive Cost Stack Table: This is an analysis that shows production costs and capacity for all companies in the industry. Your business must be included in the table. Ideally, it should be low-cost with high capacity, which is a first-quartile competitive position.
- Does the project have a sustainable competitive advantage, or can your leading position be reduced over time? Explain why your advantage is defensible.
- Are there strong barriers to entry that will prevent others from copying your business model? Supply a detailed explanation.

Financial Information and Economics

This is where you present the financial information and economics for the entire business or R&D project (bench testing, pilot plant, demonstration plant, first commercial plant, and full-scale implementation). If this is a startup, you must also clearly define how much capital will be needed in future periods.

You should present an extreme downside case, a conservative case, and an upside case. You will also need an explanation of all the major assumptions that were made for each scenario. This includes why the assumptions are credible, which are based on known facts, and those that will be confirmed in the project development process.

The extreme downside case is included to show that even if many of your initial assumptions go against the project, there will still be a nominal economic return.

The conservative case is a credibility statement. This should be built in such a way that all the assumptions can easily be defended.

The upside case is to paint the dream of how fantastic things could be. However, even in this case, your assumptions need to be plausible, well-defined, and defensible.

For each case, you should have a summary income statement, balance sheet, statement of cash flow, NPV, IRR, and other economic measures. The full financial statements should be in the appendix.

Other items to include are a definition of financial terms and adjustments made to the financials for one-time events (if any). Be careful with pro forma adjustments, and if possible, don't make any. If there are sizable adjustments in multiple years, this is a sign the business is struggling.

Your credibility is very much on the line in this section. Any hint that the economic assumptions are unrealistic, and the entire opportunity will be questioned. They may not understand the technology but will quickly grasp the financial modeling.

Other Potential Sources of Value

These factors could help the transaction achieve even greater success or support earnings if it does not perform as initially expected.

These free options are incredibly attractive to a financial investor and should be covered in depth.

The most important items to consider are:

- Does your technology have multiple applications in other industries? For example, if your technology is a novel water-treating system, can it also be used to solve long-standing problems in other industries? The value could be substantial. The more potential applications there are for solving difficult problems in other industries, the stronger the option value.
- Also, consider whether other sources of potential value are obvious to you but may not be clear to others. An example might be improved national security or lower-

cost raw material for other US industries. Include an explanation of these advantages in your presentation.

- Will the transaction benefit from ongoing changes in society? This is an important consideration for the venture capital company because this type of dynamic can result in entirely new and very profitable industries. Examples of future societal changes are conversion to electric cars, aging of the workforce, increased use of renewable energy, and continued expansion of social media. If a compelling case is made in this area, that may be enough to get an investor on board even when the project is in the initial stages.

Structure and Governance

Company structure and governance should be included at a high level in your materials. Sometimes this topic is excluded from the CIM in a misguided attempt to attract as many companies as possible.

However, there is no value in leaving such an important consideration for later in the process. Defining your expectations up front will help weed out unacceptable counterparties and focus your efforts on those that offer the greatest chance of success.

There is a lot to consider in this area, but at a minimum, you should include:

- **Transaction Flowchart.** This explains what each group is contributing (cash, existing investment in the business, know-how, other intellectual property such as patents, and future capital investments) and what each will receive in return (ownership or other consideration). Creating a visual drawing that shows what each party is contributing and what each party is receiving will help clarify your thinking concerning the essential components of the transaction. You should also discuss the transaction flowchart with the other party to ensure everyone is on the same page before beginning work on the term sheet.

- **Company Structure and Governance.** These are separate items but should be considered together. Some of the considerations include ownership percentages, potential dilution of your ownership over time, board of managers' voting rights and blocking rights, right to appoint managers of the venture, authority of the company's officers, ownership put and call rights using a predetermined pricing formula, payment of cash dividends, how the company will be run and a lot more.

- **Negotiation Positions.** When putting this together, you should consider which items are hard walkaway items and what you may be able to compromise on.

The counterparties will be looking for a straightforward structure with limited transaction and governance risk. This should also be your goal. Complex structures have prevented many transactions from going forward.

Also, whatever you propose must be balanced and fair. Don't stake out a lopsided position that you know will be unacceptable. This will just trigger an equally lopsided response with two negative consequences. First, the counterparty will question if your expectations are so unrealistic that it will be impossible to reach an agreement and potentially move on to other opportunities. Second, you will likely give up more value chasing the deal than if you had been fair from the beginning and simply defended your reasonable positions.

Contact Information

Contact information for your M&A consultant should be included at the end of the document.

In general, company representatives should avoid talking directly with potential purchasers or investors during the initial stages of the M&A process.

Use your M&A consultant as a communication buffer, so you can stay focused on developing the opportunity and running the business.

In addition, when it comes time to thin out the prospective counterparties or draw a hard line on issues (e.g., this is a horse race with no exclusivity), your consultant can deliver the message impartially and shield you from appeals to change your decision.

Appendix

The appendix is primarily for background information, which is useful but unlikely to change a counterparty's decision to move forward with the M&A process.

Financial statements are the exception. These must be complete and will likely be examined in detail from the start.

Other topics you should consider including in the appendix are:

- Technical Discussion and Details
- Industry Landscape
  - Markets
  - Competitors
- Business Details
  - Plant Layout
  - Operations
  - Feedstock/Raw Materials
  - Products/Marketing
  - Customers (current and potential)
  - Management
  - Technical Service
  - Compliance and Legal Services
  - Transition Services

The Documents Matter - Concluding Thoughts

The focus of this chapter is to provide further information on some of the most important M&A documents.

I encourage you to refer to this material when undertaking a transaction to help ensure all principal matters are considered.

Also, stay heavily involved in drafting the agreements (an M&A Best Practice) or prepare to pay the price.

Chapter 10
Toolbox

The Toolbox is devoted to specific tools referred to in earlier discussions that will help you during the M&A process.

Acquisition Process: Outline of Major Steps

- Primary steps associated with an acquisition in table format

Sale Process: Outline of Major Steps

- Primary steps associated with a divestiture in table format

Term Sheet Preparation: Acquisition Example

- Example of an acquisition term sheet

Transaction Flowchart Example

- This is an arrow diagram explaining the proposed transaction: what each group is contributing (e.g., IP/cash/marketing/existing business) and what they get back in the form of equity, rights, or payment.

Acquisition Process: Outline of Major Steps

Process Steps
Start with vision & strategy. Example questions might be: What are you trying to accomplish with this acquisition? Will it improve your competitive position? Will it contribute significantly to earnings growth? If you cannot answer these questions, consider completing a Vision & Strategy Reset before going further (see Chapter 4).
Screen all the assets or companies in this space. How does the target compare? Does it have a strong competitive advantage? If not, consider whether you want to proceed.
Define the universe of potential purchasers. Are you the logical purchaser? Why not? Study why others have passed on this opportunity. Are you missing something?
Consider if the proposed acquisition is consistent with your Vision & Strategy before proceeding. Just because something is for sale does not mean you should buy it.
Understand from the seller what is being sold and what is being retained. Is this division problematic?
Discuss purchase price expectations with the seller to determine if they are realistic. Decide if you want to proceed based on the response.
Select your deal team. You should have representatives from all areas of the business. It is also particularly important that the team includes people responsible for running the business to avoid handoff confusion and lack of ownership. The group should be comprised of people from commercial, operations, environmental, safety, human resources, information technology, accounting, treasury, tax, legal, business development, and M&A.
Review the seller's teaser that is sent to potential purchasers without requiring a nondisclosure agreement (NDA). This should have a moderate level of financial information for the

last three years, including the current year's EBITDA and value of inventory. It should also define anything that is excluded (e.g., debt/cash/assets/intellectual property). Are there any concerns?

Negotiate and sign the NDA if the initial teaser is sufficiently interesting to continue.

Prepare an initial list of key concerns. Every transaction has ten to fifteen due diligence items that are truly important and a lot of others that are noise. It is quite easy to get lost in the thousands of details.

To help ensure you identify the most significant items, start by reviewing the information in the CIM, data room, management presentation, and seller's draft purchase agreement. Begin the discussion with your deal team by asking them to define the three worst discoveries they could make in their area during due diligence.

These items will become the backbone of your initial list of key concerns. The list should be updated on a real-time basis by removing resolved items and including additional items of concern as more information becomes available and you learn more.

Focus your diligence on the areas of key concern by including them as headline items in your overall due diligence work plan. You should also have a standing deal team meeting at least once a week. The purpose of this meeting is not to deliver a status report but to get the group's input on areas of concern and make other members aware of items that may be important to them.

Ensure each of the key concerns, due diligence items, and economic bets are owned by someone on the deal team. Before the purchase agreements are signed, and again before the transaction is closed, each member of the deal team should give their personal "good to go" concerning the completion of their diligence items and the success of their economic bets.

Review the seller's CIM that is sent to companies that sign the NDA. This should have more financial information about the business and in-depth information about the assets or business being sold. Note what is concerning and what is missing. These items should go on the list of your key concerns.

Review the bid process letter. Are there any problems? Discuss with the seller.

Review the electronic data room. This should hold all the documents for review (e.g., contracts/licenses/permits/title policies). Sections of the data room may be opened at separate times.

For example, customer contracts and lists may not be available for viewing except in redacted form until further along in the process. Decide who will collaborate with the seller to gather and submit questions. Note what is concerning and what is missing. This information should go on your list of key concerns.

Decide which team members will review each section of the data room.

Ask the seller to supply anything that you believe is missing. Complete disclosure of all relevant information through the data room is essential.

Decide who will review the seller's answers to questions sent through the data site. You should name a subject matter expert for each area to take the lead.

Review the management presentation document provided by the seller. What is concerning, and what is missing? Develop a list of questions from the management presentation, CIM, and data room that will be asked during the in-person management meeting, and identify which person on your deal team will have the lead. Add these items to your list of key concerns.

Decide who will take part in the management presentation and site visits.
Schedule a management presentation.
Schedule site visits for your subject matter experts, such as operations and environmental.
Review the seller's draft purchase agreement for significant issues. The agreement will likely be very seller friendly, so do not try to redline the agreement. Instead, submit a term sheet that defines the major commercial and legal terms you are willing to accept.
Develop a comprehensive term sheet to ensure that you have thought through the major commercial terms associated with the transaction before discussions start with the seller and that everyone in your organization is on the same page concerning the major deal terms.
Include the following items in your term sheet: the proposed price, a definition of value that is transferred to the purchaser and retained by the seller (e.g., assets/IP), a division of liabilities between the purchaser and seller (e.g., our watch/your watch division of environmental liability), and expectations concerning the certainty of closing (e.g., no financing contingency).
Draft bid letter.
Send the bid letter and the term sheet to the seller.
Set up a call with the seller to determine if you will be moving forward to final negotiations and if you will be the only company. Ask for an honest assessment of your term sheet proposal. Is there room for a deal based on the seller's response?
Decide if you are willing to continue without exclusivity. The seller will likely bring multiple companies forward for the final round of negotiations. This supplies urgency and

177

competitive tension, which will help them get the best price and close the sale.
Negotiate a <u>final</u> term sheet with the seller. This step is needed to ensure that a true agreement has been reached on the major commercial terms before starting to draft the legal agreements. This also prevents the seller or their attorneys from attempting to re-trade the deal while the legal agreements are being drafted.
Draft the final purchase agreement using the term sheet as a guide. Negotiate any remaining items.
Sign the purchase agreement.
Begin the closing process. The seller will be required to manage and maintain the business in the normal course and complete other activities (such as assigning contracts).
Develop a funds flow statement that defines the additions and/or deductions that will be made to the purchase price and supplies wire transfer instructions. Send it to the seller and complete the document.
Send funds by wire when all closing conditions have been met and complete the sale.
Oversee post-closing matters and true-ups as required by the purchase agreement.

Sale Process: Outline of Major Steps

Process Steps
Start with Vision & Strategy. Example questions might be: – What are you trying to accomplish with this sale? – Will it improve your competitive position? – Will it contribute significantly to earnings growth? – Can you reinvest the proceeds in higher-quality assets? If you cannot answer these questions, consider completing a Vision & Strategy Reset before going further (see Chapter 4).
Screen all the assets or companies in this space. How does the asset that is being sold compare? Does it have a strong competitive advantage? Consider this when drafting the teaser and CIM.
Define the universe of potential purchasers using input from the company being sold. Exclude companies and individuals that may use the process to steal your intellectual property or clients. Integrity is important when selecting potential purchasers to move to the next step in the bidding process. Also, carefully vet foreign companies and individuals against US government databases. Define the list of logical purchasers and include them in the bidders' list.
Consider if the proposed sale is consistent with your Vision & Strategy before continuing. Just because something can be sold does not mean this is in the company's best interest.
Define what is being sold and what is being retained. Also, discuss sales price expectations. This information will not be shared with purchasers but is needed to understand if the seller has a realistic price outlook.
Select your deal team. You should have representatives from all areas of the business. It is also especially important that the team includes people currently responsible for running the business to avoid handoff confusion and lack of ownership.

The group should be made up of people from commercial, operations, environmental, safety, human resources, information technology, accounting, treasury, tax, legal, business development, and M&A.
Prepare the financial information that will be contained in the teaser.
Formulate an initial teaser that can be sent to potential purchasers without needing an NDA. This would have a moderate level of financial information for the last three years, including the current year (e.g., EBITDA/value of inventory), and define anything that is excluded (e.g., debt/cash/assets/intellectual property).
Send the initial teaser to potential purchasers and follow up by phone to determine their interest.
Develop a CIM that would be sent to companies that sign an NDA. This would have more financial information (income statement/balance sheet if selling stock/cash flow statement) and information about the assets or business being sold.
Vet the companies and officers against government databases and use an outside firm to complete a high-level background check before sending the nondisclosure agreement (NDA) to potential purchasers.
Send and negotiate NDAs with interested companies.
Forward the CIM and follow up concerning interest. Indicate you will be sending a bid process letter and term sheet.
Build an electronic data room. This will hold all documents for review (e.g., contracts/licenses/permits/deeds/title policies). Sections of the data room can be opened to purchasers at separate times.
For example, customer contracts and lists would not be available for viewing until the end of the process. Decide who will collaborate with the purchasers to gather and review documents, administer the site (upload documents), and supply a legal review before they are loaded. Decide if any

information is subject to US Export Controls and manage it appropriately.
Include <u>all</u> relevant information in the data room. Complete disclosure is especially important. Do not hold anything back, or you could be accused of fraud.
Decide who will review questions from the purchasers, develop answers to the questions (seller's subject matter experts), and provide a legal review of the answers before they are released.
Draft a bid process letter and set a date for the initial bid.
Open data room to purchasers that have signed an NDA.
Answer questions sent by the purchasers.
Develop a term sheet of four-to-five pages that defines the major commercial and legal terms associated with the transaction. This is important because the purchasers will consider these provisions when sending their bids. Creating this document also helps the seller think through the main commercial terms associated with the transaction before discussions start with the purchasers.   The document should have a blank space for purchase price, definition of value that is transferred (e.g., assets/stock), division of liabilities between purchaser and seller (e.g., our watch/your watch division of environmental liability), and expectations concerning the certainty of the close (e.g., no financing contingency).
Send a bid process letter and the term sheet to the purchasers.
Decide who will be present at site visits from both the seller and the deal team.
Schedule site visits.
Determine if you will have a management presentation and which of the seller's people will be presenting (only needed for large transactions).

Prepare the management presentation document.
Send the management presentation document to the bidders.
Schedule in-person management presentations.
Receive bids from the purchasers and evaluate based on price, changes to the term sheet, and other relevant factors. Decide which bidders to bring forward for final negotiations.
Start the horse race. Indicate you are taking multiple companies forward, and the winner will be the first company across the line with the best price and terms. This supplies urgency and competitive tension, which is important to get the best price and close the sale.
Begin by simultaneously negotiating a <u>final</u> term sheet with each of the remaining bidders.
Select the bidder with the best price and most attractive term sheet.
Notify the lead bidder they are moving forward to draft binding legal agreements.
Draft the purchase agreement using the most favorable term sheet as a guide. Negotiate any remaining items.
Sign the purchase agreement.
Begin the closing process. The seller will be required to manage and maintain the business in the normal course and complete other activities (such as assigning contracts if not a stock sale).
Prepare a funds flow statement that defines the additions and/or deductions that will be made to the price and supplies wire transfer instructions. Send it to the purchaser and complete the document.
Receive funds by wire and complete the sale when all closing conditions are met.

Manage post-closing matters and true-ups as required by the purchase agreement.

Term Sheet Preparation
Acquisition Example

_____, 20__

The following outlines the key terms that would be included in the Asset Purchase Agreement ("APA") between _____ and _____ (Collectively "Seller") and _____ with its newly formed affiliate _____ (Collectively "Purchaser").

The Purchaser is pleased to submit this nonbinding indication of interest to acquire the assets of the Seller. In submitting this indication of interest, we have relied primarily on the Confidential Information Memorandum ("CIM") and the Seller's Data Room. Capitalized terms used in this letter without definition have the meanings assigned to them in the CIM.

Structure

The transaction would be structured as an Asset Purchase by the Purchaser of all the Seller's assets that are used or useful in the Business as described in the CIM.

Price Paid

Purchase Price: We are prepared to value the Seller's Business on a cash-free/debt-free basis at _____ million ("Purchase Price").

In addition to the Purchase Price, we are prepared to offer additional value in the form of an earn-out ("Earn-Out") of up to $_____ million, which will generally be calculated as follows:_____ .

The definitive structure and payment mechanism for the Earn-Out will be incorporated into the final agreements.

The Seller will retain accounts receivable and accounts payable.

Payment for Inventory

There will be a separate payment for the inventory of raw materials and finished products.

The price will be the lowest of the Seller's cost of production, cost of purchase, or market value.

Inventory levels will be capped at historical volumes. Any inventory above this amount at closing will transfer to the Purchaser at no cost.

Inventory will not include off-specification products, contaminated products, emulsions, BS&W, water, tank heels, or anything else that does not have market value.

Assets Acquired by Purchaser

The transaction would be structured as a purchase of all the Seller's assets that are used or useful in the Business as described in the Confidential Information Memorandum and Management Presentation, as well as everything that was used or necessary to operate the business, run the plants, import raw materials, blend products, and market products, over the past twenty-four months, including but not limited to the following:

- Production facilities
- Process units
- Equipment
- Buildings
- Tanks
- Pipelines
- Trucks
- Truck loading facilities
- Rail loading facilities
- Catalyst
- Chemicals
- Packaging
- Spare parts
- Real property and buffer property, owned or leased

- Right-of-way agreements, easements, permits
- Contracts, agreements
- Government licenses and permits
- IP, patents, formulas, know-how
- Brand names, trademarks, domain names
- Rolling stock, vehicles, rail cars
- Computers and software
- Data, records, plans, manuals, drawings, specifications
- Customer lists, marketing studies
- Strategic studies
- Tangible personal property
- Buildings

Assets Retained by Seller (Excluded Assets)

The Seller will not retain any assets. This includes but is not limited to the following:

- Real property
- Process units
- Blending equipment
- Buildings located on or off real property
- Surrounding land and buffer property
- Intellectual Property
- Rights to Seller's Brand
- Spare parts

Debt and Liens

All outstanding indebtedness of Seller will be repaid at closing, and the Purchased Assets will be free and clear of all liens and encumbrances other than agreed-upon permitted liens and encumbrances.

Liabilities Assumed by Purchaser

Purchaser will assume only limited contractual liabilities that are necessary to operate the Business after closing.

Purchaser will assume no other liabilities of Seller.

Liabilities Retained by Seller

The Seller will retain all liabilities from pre-closing matters, including but not limited to the following:

- Environmental contamination (known and unknown)
- Natural resource damage claims
- Superfund claims
- Pre-closing violations of environmental, health, and safety laws and any violations discovered within twelve months after closing
- Pre-closing violations of antitrust laws discovered within six months after closing
- Off-site disposal of hazardous and non-hazardous waste
- Products sold before closing
- Contracts and permits that are not transferred
- Taxes
- Accounts payable
- Debt and liens
- Employee benefit plans and employee matters, including severance payments
- Claims arising out of the pre-closing condition of the plants
- Liabilities associated with prior acquisitions and dispositions
- Seller obligations to shareholders, partners, and investors

Representations and Warranties

The Seller shall make representations and warranties customary for similar transactions. This includes but is not limited to the following:

- The Purchaser will receive everything necessary to conduct Business in the normal course as it's been operated in the last twenty-four months.
- The assets are in good operating condition and have been maintained in accordance with standard industry practice.

- The company's financial statements are materially correct and prepared in accordance with GAAP.
- The assets and business have complied with all laws, rules, and regulations, including environmental laws.
- The plant production capacities shown in the Confidential Information Memorandum and Management Presentation can be achieved and sustained when the operations are running in the normal course of business.
- The storage capacity shown in the Confidential Information Memorandum and Management Presentation can be achieved and sustained when the operations are running in the normal course of business.
- The sales capacity shown in the Confidential Information Memorandum and Management Presentation can be achieved and sustained when the operations are running in the normal course of business.
- The Seller has the necessary power to complete the transaction.

Exceptions to these representations and warranties will be shown on a separate disclosure schedule.

Fundamental Representations and Warranties

Seller and Purchaser shall make fundamental representations and warranties customary for similar transactions, including but not limited to the following:

- Organization, Power, and Authorization
- No Conflicts
- No Broker or Finder's Fee
- Title to Assets

Indemnity

- Seller will indemnify Purchaser for any loss, including attorney's fees related to:

  o Retained liabilities
  o Any breach of Seller's reps and warranties for the associated survival period

- o Seller's breach of any of its covenants; and
- o Any fraud or intentional misrepresentation by the Seller
- Purchaser will indemnify Seller for any loss, including attorney's fees related to:
  - o Assumed liabilities
  - o Any breach of Purchaser's reps and warranties for the associated survival period
  - o Purchaser's breach of any of its covenants; and
  - o Any fraud or intentional misrepresentation by the Purchaser
- The indemnity for breaches of the representations and warranties will be capped at twenty percent of the purchase price.
- The indemnity for breaches of the fundamental representations will be capped at the full purchase price.
- The indemnification for retained liabilities and breaches of covenants will be uncapped and without a time limit.

Due Diligence

The Purchaser will conduct Phase I environmental assessments at all of the Seller's facilities. Based on the findings, the Purchaser may decide to conduct Phase II environmental assessments on all or some of the Seller's facilities.

This indication of interest is contingent upon completion to our sole satisfaction of business, financial, legal, accounting, environmental, and other customary due diligence for a transaction of this nature. We anticipate the process will take _____ days from the date Purchaser is granted exclusivity at the end of the second round of bidding. This assumes the Seller promptly provides all necessary information, access to senior management, and access to the site.

We anticipate that our due diligence investigation will require a review of the following items as well as other information related to the Seller and the Business as we may request.

- Everything that is listed in a Schedule or Exhibit to the Asset Purchase Agreement
- Audited financial statements for three years beginning on 20_
- Interim current-year financial statements provided on a monthly basis
- Liabilities from prior acquisitions completed by the Seller
- Listing of all liabilities on the Seller's Balance Sheet
- Seller's stockholder agreements
- Full and complete access to facilities
- Access to knowledgeable company personnel
- Access to Seller's management and employees as required for follow-up questions generated from due diligence
- Plant operation and production logs for twenty-four months
- All environmental licenses and permits
- Existing Phase I reports, Phase II reports, and environmental insurance policies, plus all other environmental-related reports or plans, including SPCC plans, site characterization reports for open environmental items, Notice of Violations, and all NFA letters and closure reports for past environmental incidents
- All contracts and leases with amounts in excess of $____ million per year and all contracts with take or pay provisions
- All marketing and sales agreements in excess of $_____ thousand per year
- Historical inventory volumes by month for the last two years
- Pipeline right-of-way agreements
- All agreements and leases associated with company equipment and vehicles
- Land title and lease agreements

HR Matters

Purchaser will interview and make offers of employment to certain of Seller's management and nonmanagement employees. As part of this process, the Purchaser will conduct background checks and drug screenings.

The Seller will terminate all the remaining employees as a part of the closing process, and any severance payment will be the responsibility of the Seller.

Conduct of Business: Covenants

The Seller will be required to:

- Operate the business in the ordinary course.
- Maintain the assets in their current condition, including making planned capital and maintenance expenditures.
- Comply with applicable laws.
- Not sell or dispose of any material assets.
- Not add debt or liens.
- Not cancel or change any material contract or permit.
- Not issue or grant additional equity or stock.

Regulatory Approvals

Purchaser and Seller will work together to secure any regulatory approvals for the transaction.

Parent Guarantee

_____will provide a Parent Guarantee to ensure the Seller meets its obligations under the agreement.

_____will provide a Parent Guarantee to ensure the Purchaser meets its obligations under the agreement.

Closing Conditions

The Purchaser's closing of the transaction will be conditioned upon the following:

- Customary government and regulatory approvals have been received.

- Permits necessary to operate the facilities have been transferred or acquired.
- Consents for certain material contracts have been received.
- Debt has been repaid and liens removed.
- Casualty loss above a certain amount has been cured.
- Accuracy of Seller's representations and warranties has been verified.
- Seller is in compliance with covenants and other agreements in the transaction documents.
- No material adverse effect (MAE) has occurred or is likely to occur.
- All facilities and equipment are operating at normal rates.
- Approval of the Seller's stockholders (if required) should be completed before signing the definitive agreements rather than a closing condition.
- Approval by the seller's board of managers or board of directors should be completed before signing the definitive agreements rather than a closing condition.

Termination

Termination provisions will include the following:

- If closing has not occurred by a specific date (Outside Date in final agreements)
- Declaration of bankruptcy by either party

Liquidated Damages Break Fee

Either party can terminate the Transaction with no further obligation to the other party by making a $_____ million liquidated damages payment to the other party at any time before closing.

Other Agreements

The following additional agreements need to be included in the transaction documents:

- Transition Services

- Use of Seller's Brand (exclusive, perpetual, and royalty-free)
- Intellectual property licenses (exclusive, perpetual, and without fee)
- Noncompete Agreement

Board Approval

- Seller and Purchaser will secure Board approval when the term sheet is agreed upon.
- Seller and Purchaser will acquire formal written Board approval before signing the definitive agreements.

Stockholder Support Agreement

- Approval of Seller's Stockholders (if required) should be completed before signing the definitive agreements rather than as a closing condition

  o Approve the Transaction.
  o Amend or waive provisions in the Shareholder Agreement as necessary to facilitate the proposed Transaction.

Assignment

Purchaser will have the option to assign all or part of the purchase agreement to a future purchaser of the assets without the Seller's consent. This includes the Seller's indemnities.

Legal Matters

This section of the Term Sheet is added as a second step only after the major commercial terms have been agreed upon.

Transaction Flowchart Example

Creating a visual drawing that shows what each party is contributing and what each party is receiving will help clarify your thinking concerning the essential components of the transaction.

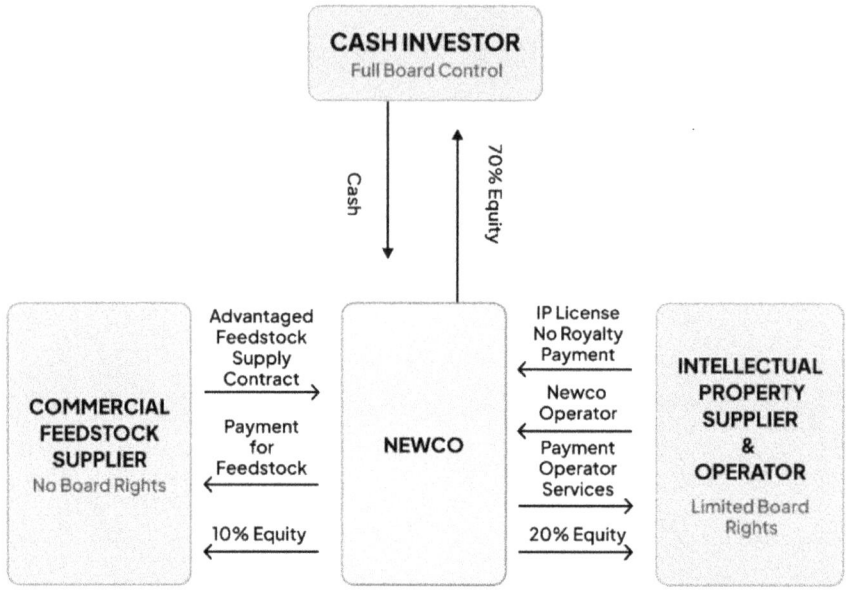

Chapter 11
Application Is Unlimited

The Strategy Reset and M&A Best Practices discussed in this book have helped widely diverse companies develop dynamic new visions, execute actionable strategies, and complete highly successful transactions that have created billions of dollars in value.

Now that you have been through the book, I recommend you reexamine the case studies originally covered in Chapter 4: Vision & Strategy Reset, through the lens of your new knowledge and perspective.

For your convenience, the case studies are included below for easy reference.

Take your time reviewing the material and answer the following questions:

1) **Are the best practices demonstrated by these case studies limited to a particular industry or type of company?** To help answer this question, the case studies are listed below by industry.

Lubricants

Conoco Lubricants, a Division of Conoco, Inc:
A Fortune 500 Company

Petroleum Refining

Clark Refining and Marketing, Inc: Owned by Private Equity

Refining, Chemicals, and Biofuels

Flint Hills Resources, LLC: Subsidiary of Koch Industries, Inc

Community Services and Health Clubs

Greater Wichita YMCA: Nonprofit

Disaster Recovery

Advance Catastrophe Technologies (ACT): Privately Held

New Technology

New Technology Startup: Confidential

Advisory

Personey M&A Advisory: Owned by the Author

2) **Which best practices are demonstrated in each of the case studies? Why are they significant?** A partial list is shown below to get you started.

> *Reset your Vision & Strategy before beginning any M&A activity.*
> *Reset your Vision & Strategy in response to competitive pressure.*
> *Develop your Vision & Strategy before entering a new industry.*
> *Consider Long-Term Macro Perspectives when developing your vision and strategy.*
> *Rationalize facilities that have a fourth-quartile competitive position.*
> *Use a joint venture to "acquire" a strongly competitive new business.*
> *Develop a fact-based competitive screening tool.*
> *Use qualitative screening analysis.*
> *Involve your employees in running the business; they know how to improve cash flow.*
> *Optimize your existing business before you begin.*
> *Improve raw material feedstock supply and purchasing costs.*
> *Enhance your product distribution network.*
> *Take advantage of your unique strengths.*
> *Understand your competitors' strengths, products, and strategies.*
> *Evaluate all potential markets for your products.*
> *Take reasonable positions, be honest and direct, and listen carefully to the other party.*
> *Ensure your vision and strategy are unique and difficult to duplicate.*

Lubricants

Conoco Lubricants, a Division of Conoco, Inc: A Fortune 500 Company

Conoco's lubricants division had marginal profitability, average product quality, inefficient operations, and high-cost base oil supply when I joined the group.

Problems existed in the entire value chain, starting with base oil production through packaging and distribution of the finished lubricants.

Our first action was to build a model of the entire blending and packaging system, which allowed us to see the cost of the finished products delivered to customers from every supply source. Nothing like this existed in Conoco at the time.

From this model, it became clear we needed to drive down the cost of our finished products delivered to the customer. We attacked this problem in the following ways:

- ➤ Some of the blending and packaging facilities were more cost-effective than others. With this information, we closed one in-house facility, built another closer to our customer base, closed some contract packagers, and expanded the volume blended by others. These changes dramatically reduced our finished lubricant production costs.
- ➤ The cost of lubricant additives and packaging materials was reduced by requiring suppliers to bid on the contracts. Something as simple as this resulted in significant savings.
- ➤ The distribution network was revamped to send products from whichever facility could deliver to the customer at the lowest overall cost. This change significantly improved margins.

This left the problem of what to do about average product quality that was not keeping up with changes in the marketplace and high-cost base oil supply. We reset the vision for sourcing base oil feedstock to address this.

The final Vision & Strategy Reset was to "Build World-Scale Production Capacity," which relied on Conoco's strength in petroleum refining. This was realized by:

> Constructing a new type of base oil manufacturing unit (lubricant hydrocracker) that produced superior products from low-cost crude oil.
> Forming a joint venture with Pennzoil to achieve world-scale size and lower production costs. The Excel Paralubes joint venture was expected to be a first-quartile facility.
> Shutting down uncompetitive base oil manufacturing units (Conoco) and uncompetitive refineries (Pennzoil).

The result was a complete turnaround in the lubricant division's profitability due to much lower operating costs, lower base oil costs, and a significant improvement in product quality. The strategy was unique and difficult for competitors to duplicate because:

> A large capital investment was needed to build a world-scale base oil lubricant hydrocracker facility. This cost was well beyond what most of the independent refining companies could manage.
> The new hydrocracking unit was designed around state-of-the-art technology, which required an extensive level of refining expertise to build and operate. This precluded most of the independent oil companies.
> The hydrocracking technology allowed the use of low-cost raw material (feedstocks) derived from heavy sour crude oil. This ruled out all the refineries (both majors and independents) that ran more expensive light crude oil.
> Conoco and Pennzoil both had small, inefficient base oil units that could be shut down to supply initial product demand. This was not the case for most major oil companies.

Petroleum Refining

Clark Refining and Marketing, Inc: Owned by Private Equity

Clark had marginal profitability, small, uncompetitive refineries, and was just emerging from bankruptcy when I joined the company.

Refining margins were at an all-time low, no new refining capacity was being built, uncompetitive refineries were being shut down, and the major oil companies were selling refineries.

The first thing I did was undertake the development of a model that would project the expected profitability for every refinery in the United States. It was built around a linear program using publicly available information.

The development of the model was an enormous success. It allowed us to screen all available acquisition targets against the universe of competitors in the industry to identify the facilities with a first and second-quartile competitive position.

The model was called the "Prism System," and, at the time, nothing like it was available in the US refining industry or from refining consultants.

The results of the model made it clear that radical change was required for the company to survive in the long term. The existing refineries were simply not competitive. Equally important, the Prism System also helped identify which refineries might be good acquisition candidates.

The first thing we did was optimize our existing refineries so the company could operate at cash flow breakeven under the worst market conditions.

This was done by tapping into the latent knowledge of employees concerning how to improve the current operations. With our employees' ideas and help, we materially improved cash flow despite a very difficult business environment.

This left the problem of how to upgrade our refinery assets.
To address this, we reset the vision by moving away from an
operating company mentality and taking advantage of the M&A
capability brought to the company by new owners and officers.
With this new capability, we transformed into a growth
company.

**The final Vision & Strategy Reset was to "Survive and
Acquire."** This was realized by:

> ➢ Recognizing that margins could not stay at current levels
> for an extended period; as demand grew and capacity
> was rationalized, margins would recover
> ➢ Recognizing that some of the majors were not running
> their facilities to maximize profitability (sub-optimizing
> their plants and incurring higher costs than needed)
> ➢ Using the Prism System to identify potential acquisition
> candidates. We were looking for refineries that screened
> well but had poor earnings as operated by the current
> owner

This offered an opportunity to acquire refineries that were being
sold by the majors at deep discounts and improve their
operations.

The Chevron Port Arthur refinery was identified this way,
purchased for $76 million plus inventory, quickly turned
around, and was valued at $2–3 billion within several years.

**This acquisition resulted in a complete reversal of Clark's
profitability** and prospects. The strategy was unique and
difficult for competitors to duplicate because:

> ➢ It required a point of view that refining margins would
> improve in three to five years. The majors did not believe
> this because margins had been at historic lows for several
> years, and the independents were afraid to take the risk.
> ➢ Clark's existing refineries could be shut down or sold
> without a material loss of earnings because of their poor
> competitive position. This option was not available to
> other potential purchasers.

> ➤ Clark was running at cash flow breakeven to survive until margins improved. This required tapping into the latent knowledge of all employees concerning what changes could be made and having the organizational will to follow it through.
> ➤ The Port Arthur refinery had negative cash flow and needed to make significant changes. The majors were unwilling to take the risk, and the independents lacked the skills needed to recognize what was required.

Refining, Chemicals, and Biofuels

Flint Hills Resources, LLC: Subsidiary of Koch Industries, Inc

The company had strong refining assets, favorable geographic locations, and reasonable profitability despite significant pressure on refining margins when I joined the company.

Refining margins remained at an all-time low, no new refining capacity was being built, uncompetitive refineries were being shut down, and many of the best refining assets in the United States had already come to market and had been sold.

The first thing we did was optimize the existing refineries so the company could justify new M&A growth.

This was a companywide effort focused on improving profitability and was referred to as the "Call to Action."

With ideas and help from employees across the company, we were able to materially improve earnings, which set the stage for significant capital investment in our existing refineries as well as new M&A activity.

This left the problem of where to focus our acquisitions. To address this, we reset the entire vision of the company by moving away from a pure refining platform and transforming into a diversified refining, chemicals, and biofuels company.

The final Vision & Strategy Reset was to "Acquire New Business Platforms." This was realized by:

> ➤ Purchasing other types of heavy manufacturing facilities that were experiencing depressed margins and that FHR could run with their refining capability
> ➤ Focusing on buying chemical manufacturing facilities that had depressed prices and ethanol plants with competitive advantages
> ➤ Acquiring Huntsman's Base Chemicals and Polymers business for $770 million (public filing) and materially improving the operation (the ethylene part of the

business was sold in 2020, but the purchase price was not disclosed).

This strategy resulted in substantial growth in the company's profitability and capability. The strategy was unique and difficult for competitors to duplicate because:

➢ Huntsman's Olefin Cracker, located in Port Arthur, Texas, had experienced a major fire and was being repaired while the sale process was underway. This was too much risk for the management at major oil companies, as well as too much risk for independent oil companies because failure of the repair project could jeopardize their entire company. After a thorough evaluation, we concluded the repair project was well run and included startup requirements in the Asset Purchase Agreement to help mitigate the risk.

➢ Flint Hills Resources continued making changes to improve the existing refining operations and reduce costs while at the same time absorbing the new acquisitions. This required tapping into the latent knowledge of all employees, including those who came with the acquisitions.

➢ Flint Hills Resources was uniquely positioned to accomplish this due to the Market-Based Management capability, which is a part of all Koch Industries companies.

Community Services and Health Clubs

Greater Wichita YMCA: Nonprofit

This nonprofit company had high-quality facilities and stable profitability when I started my advisory engagement.

However, increased competitive pressure was coming from low-cost providers and digital exercise platforms. Also, there was a high turnover of first-time members who didn't feel connected or use the facilities on a routine basis.

Building more facilities—the existing strategy—did not address these concerns.

The YMCA offers a broad range of activities, including exercise classes, swimming, basketball, nutrition classes, youth sports, SilverSneakers, weightlifting, and martial arts, all of which have talented instructors.

The best way to address these concerns and take advantage of the YMCA's unique strengths was to reset the vision of the company.

The final Vision & Strategy Reset was to "Build Community." This was realized by:

> ➤ Creating a <u>digital</u> community to reach people who will not go to the brick-and-mortar facilities but would like to access the content and increase the retention of new members.
> ➤ Offering existing members access to the new digital programming.

The Strategy Reset received enthusiastic support from both the local business community and other YMCA franchises.

The strategy was introduced to the public as "YMCA 360" just before the pandemic and has been a remarkable success. This strategy was unique and difficult for competitors to duplicate because:

- ➢ The digital platform includes a large part of the YMCA's extremely broad and diverse offerings. No other competitor can offer a similar range of activities.
- ➢ The platform includes the YMCA's high-quality influencers, many of whom are well-known. This ensures an immediate member following for the digital offerings and strong future growth in users.
- ➢ Content on the site is being contributed by YMCA organizations from across the United States. Worldwide the YMCA serves forty-five million people and is found in 10,000 communities in the United States. No other competitor comes close to matching this breadth of potential digital content or market access.

Disaster Recovery

Advance Catastrophe Technologies: Privately Held

This company had stable profitability but limited earnings growth potential when I started my advisory engagement.

The strength of Advance Catastrophe Technologies (ACT) was disaster recovery in the hospitality business (e.g., hotels), a narrow subset of the entire disaster recovery industry.

They also did not have many brick-and-mortar offices spread across the United States.

The best way to address these concerns and take advantage of ACT's unique strengths was to reset the vision of the company.

The final Vision & Strategy Reset was to "Create Value for the Customer." This was realized by:

> ➢ Deploying mobile Critical Response Units (CRUs) where they are needed most, rather than relying on brick-and-mortar offices. The CRUs can be moved to the most profitable geographic regions or quickly shifted to areas with an ongoing disaster emergency, such as a hurricane, record low temperatures, or wildfires.
> ➢ Leading the adoption of new disaster recovery technology to improve the customers' experience.
> ➢ Introducing new client-focused services such as insurance support.
> ➢ Penetrating new markets by creating focused value propositions for the customer supported by internal champions.

Implementing these strategies materially improved profitability and created significant growth potential. This strategy was unique and difficult for competitors to duplicate because:

> ➢ The larger competitors are heavily invested in brick-and-mortar locations that lock them into high-cost office

space and specific geographic regions. In contrast, ACT's CRUs are mobile. They can be moved to the most profitable geographic regions or quickly shifted to areas with an ongoing disaster emergency to better serve their customers.

➤ The first mover in the use of innovative technology will command customer loyalty. This requires an ongoing entrepreneurial focus, which is difficult for many companies to sustain, and that ACT has undertaken.

➤ Regional focus is the predominant business model for most companies in the disaster recovery industry. Instead, ACT will use vertical champions to bring expertise to target nationwide segments of the market. Customers value this added experience.

New Technology

New Technology Startup: Confidential

This privately held company had a stable business model but limited upside potential when I started my advisory engagement.

The company's strengths were its low operating costs and established relationships in its industry.

Competitors viewed them as a niche provider for a narrow range of services. However, they also had a very innovative idea for a new product line that was not available in the market.

The best way to address these concerns and take advantage of the company's unique strengths was to reset the vision of the company.

The final Vision & Strategy Reset was realized by:

> ➢ Developing an entirely new type of product that has the potential to disrupt the entire industry. The new product would be complementary to their existing product line.
> ➢ Offering advisory services using data from the new device for an added charge.
> ➢ Penetrating the market by initially rolling out the product in the local region and then rapidly expanding from there.

Implementing these strategies is underway and is expected to result in significant upside in profitability. This strategy is unique and difficult for competitors to duplicate because:

> ➢ The new product is materially less expensive than its competitors' offerings. This opens a whole new market of smaller customers who previously did not have access to this level of expertise.
> ➢ The new product may also be attractive to larger customers because existing suppliers cannot match the prices offered by the company and remain profitable.
> ➢ This technology is entirely new, with a significant development cycle.

> ➤ The company has an advantage that will help them lock in customers by being the first to market this innovative technology.

Advisory

Personey M&A Advisory: Owned by the Author

This was a startup advisory company focused on helping companies with vision, strategy, and M&A activities.

The business was founded on three new concepts developed over forty years of professional experience. All advisory work is built on these guiding principles:

> ➤ Vision & Strategy should be the starting point for all M&A activity, including acquisitions, divestitures, mergers, and joint ventures.
> ➤ When using M&A Best Practices, it is possible to reset the Vision & Strategy of a company, identify and complete the most attractive transactions, and generate exceptional results.
> ➤ Building your firm's vision, strategy, and M&A capability will create long-term value.

This Vision & Strategy is unique and difficult for competitors to duplicate because:

> ➤ The founder has unique experience, knowledge, and skills that allow them to recognize and utilize proven M&A Best Practices in their advisory work.
> ➤ The capability needed to provide vision, strategy, and M&A advice rarely exists in the same person.
> ➤ Other advisors may prefer to charge significant fees for their services rather than teach their clients how to do the work. Their fees can be as high as six percent of an M&A transaction. This is not in the best interests of their clients.

The Upside Is Unlimited

The best practices discussed in these case studies can be applied to any business, including yours.

They represent a *very small fraction* of all the Vision, Strategy, and M&A Best Practices available to you in this book. The upside is unlimited.

This breadth of knowledge gives you the ability to take action in any situation and in any industry.

The circumstances for each company will be different, but the best practices are universally applicable in all situations.

Without a doubt, they will help you improve your success and create significant new value.

Chapter 12
Your Opportunity

Now is your opportunity to make a significant difference in the company's prospects and the lives of the people who work there!

When you embrace and use these M&A Best Practices, it will be possible to reset the Vision & Strategy of your company, identify and complete the most attractive transactions, generate exceptional results, and simultaneously build capability in your firm.

You will be shocked and pleasantly surprised at what you can accomplish using the principles and techniques discussed in this book.

They are based on over forty years of experience leading transactions, negotiating agreements, developing successful strategies, and building vision, strategy, and M&A capability.

You can be certain they will also work for you.

If you would like assistance using the concepts and principles in this book, please contact me through my company website, which you can find using the link below or by searching for **Personey M&A Consulting** on the internet.

You can also connect with me by telephone at 316-619-7868 to discuss what you would like assistance with.

Start your journey toward new vision, strategy, and M&A success today!

Glenn Personey
Founder
Personey M&A, LLC
316-619-7868
https://www.personeymallc.com